information technology

The Career Ideas for Teens Series

Career Ideas for Teens in Agriculture, Food, and Natural Resources

Career Ideas for Teens in Architecture and Construction, Second Edition

Career Ideas for Teens in the Arts and Communications, Second Edition

Career Ideas for Teens in Business, Management, and Administration

Career Ideas for Teens in Education and Training, Second Edition

Career Ideas for Teens in Finance

Career Ideas for Teens in Government and Public Service, Second Edition

Career Ideas for Teens in Health Science, Second Edition

Career Ideas for Teens in Hospitality and Tourism

Career Ideas for Teens in Human Services

Career Ideas for Teens in Information Technology, Second Edition

Career Ideas for Teens in Law and Public Safety, Second Edition

Career Ideas for Teens in Manufacturing, Second Edition

Career Ideas for Teens in Marketing

Career Ideas for Teens in Science, Technology, Engineering, and Math

Career Ideas for Teens in Transportation, Distribution, and Logistics

CAREER IDEAS for teens in

information technology

Second Edition

Diane Lindsey Reeves
and Gail Karlitz

Ferguson's
An Infobase Learning Company

Career Ideas for Teens in Information Technology, Second Edition

Copyright © 2012 by Bright Futures Press

Ferguson's
An imprint of Infobase Learning
132 West 31st Street
New York NY 10001

Library of Congress Cataloging-in-Publication Data
Reeves, Diane Lindsey, 1959-
    Career ideas for teens in information technology / Diane Lindsey Reeves and Gail Karlitz. — [2nd ed.].
        p. cm.
    Includes bibliographical references and index.
    ISBN-13: 978-0-8160-8267-4 (hardcover : acid-free paper)
    ISBN-10: 0-8160-8267-7 (hardcover : acid-free paper) 1. Information technology—Vocational guidance—Juvenile literature. 2. Computer science—Vocational guidance—Juvenile literature. I. Title.
    T58.5.R43 2012
    004.023—dc23   2011023897

Ferguson's books are available at special discounts when purchased in bulk quantities for businesses, associations, institutions, or sales promotions. Please call our Special Sales Department in New York at (212) 967-8800 or (800) 322-8755.

You can find Ferguson's on the World Wide Web at http://www.infobaselearning.com

Text design and composition by Annie O'Donnell
Cover design by Takeshi Takahashi
Illustrations by Matt Wood
Cover printed by IBT Global, Troy, N.Y.
Book printed and bound by IBT Global, Troy, N.Y.
Date printed: December 2011

Printed in the United States of America

10 9 8 7 6 5 4 3 2 1

This book is printed on acid-free paper.

CONTENTS

Welcome to Your Future   1

SECTION ONE: Discover You at Work   5

Me, Myself, and I   7
Discover #1: WHO Am I?   8
Discover #2: WHAT Do I Like to Do?   10
Discover #3: WHERE Does My Work Style Fit Best?   12
Discover #4: WHY Do My Work Values Matter?   17
Discover #5: HOW Ready Am I for the 21st-Century Workplace?   20
Discover #6: "Me" Résumé   25

Hello, World of Work   26
Discover #7: WHERE Can My Interests and Skills Take Me?   26
Discover #8: WHICH Career Path Is Right for Me?   37
Discover #9: Career Résumé   41

SECTION TWO: Explore Your Options   43
Applications Developer   47
Artificial Intelligence Scientist   50
Business Intelligence Analyst   53
Chief Information Officer   56
Computer Programmer   59
Computer Repair Technician   62
Cyber Intelligence Analyst   65
Database Administrator   68
Database Modeler   71
Data Visualization Specialist   74
Digital Forensics Expert   77
Disaster Recovery Analyst   80
E-Commerce Entrepreneur   83
Hardware Engineer   86

Health Informatics Specialist   89
Information Security Specialist   92
Information Technology Auditor   95
Information Technology Consultant   98
Information Technology Project Manager   101
Intrusion Detection Analyst   104
Network Administrator   107
Robotics Software Engineer   110
Robotics Technologist   113
Search Engine Optimization Specialist   116
Simulation Designer   119
Social Media Manager   122
Software Quality Assurance Analyst   125
Systems Analyst   128
Technical Support Specialist   131
Technical Writer   134
3-D Computer Animator   137
Usability Specialist   140
Video Game Designer   143
Video Game Sound Designer   146
Webmaster   149

SECTION THREE: Experiment with Success   153
ASK for Advice and Start Building a
   Career-Boosting Network   155
ASSESS a Variety of Workplace Options   161
ADDRESS Options to Make the Most of Now   168

A Final Word   173
Appendix   175
Index   182

Welcome to Your Future

Q: What is one of the most dreaded questions of the high school experience?

A: What are you going to do after you graduate?

Talk about pressure! You have to come up with an answer sometime soon. But, homecoming is right around the corner; coach called an extra practice; homework is piling up....

Feel free to delay the inevitable. But here's the deal: Sooner or later the same people who make you go to school now are eventually going to make you stop. If you get it right, you'll exit with diploma in hand and at least a general idea of what to do next.

So...

What *are* you going to do after you graduate?

There are plenty of choices. You could go away to college or give community college a try; get a job or enlist in the military. Maybe you can convince your parents to bankroll an extended break to travel the world. Or, perhaps, you want to see what's out there by volunteering for a favorite cause or interning with an interesting company.

Of course, you may be one of the lucky few who have always known what they wanted to do with their lives—be a doctor, chef, or whatever. All you need to do is figure out a few wheres, whens, and hows to get you on your way. Get the training, master the skills, and off you go to fulfill your destiny.

On the other hand, you may be one of the hordes of high schoolers who have absolutely no clue what they want to do with the rest of their lives. But—whatever—you'll just head off to college anyway. After all, everyone else is doing it. And, for that matter, everyone that matters seems to think that's what you're *supposed* to do.

But, here's the thing: College is pretty much a once-in-a-life-time opportunity. Not to mention that it is a *very expensive* once-in-a-lifetime-opportunity. It's unlikely that you'll ever get another four years to step back from the rest of the world and totally focus on getting yourself ready to succeed in life. Assuming that you are way too smart to squander your best shot at success with aimless dabbling, you can use this book to make well-informed choices about your future.

A premise suggested by a famous guy named Noel Coward inspired the ultimate goal of this book. Coward was an English playwright who was born in 1899. After a colorful life working as a composer, director, actor, and singer, Coward concluded that interesting "work is more fun than fun." Making this statement true for you is what this book is all about.

Mind you, fun isn't limited to the ha-ha, goofing-off-with-friends variety. Sometimes it's best expressed as the big sigh of satisfaction people describe when they truly enjoy their life's work. It involves finding the kind of work that provides purpose to your days and a solid foundation for building a well-rounded life. You'll know you've found it when you look forward to Mondays almost as much as you do Fridays!

Need more convincing? Consider this: If you are like most people, you will spend a big chunk of the next 40 or 50 years of your life working. Sorry to break it to you like that but, well, welcome to the real world. Putting a little thought into how you really want to spend all that time kind of makes sense, doesn't it?

If you agree, you've come to the right place. In these pages you'll encounter a sequence of activities and strategies you can use—much like a compass—to find your way to a bright future. Each of the 16 titles in the *Career Ideas for Teens* series features the following three sections:

SECTION ONE: DISCOVER YOU AT WORK

It's your choice, your career, your future. Do you notice a common theme here? Yep, this first step is all about you. Stop here and

WHICH WAY SHOULD YOU GO?

Each of the 16 titles in the *Career Ideas for Teens* series focus on a specific industry theme. Some people refer to these themes as career "clusters." Others call them career "pathways." Your school may even offer career academies based on one or more of these themes. Whatever you call them, they offer a terrific way to explore the entire world of work in manageable, easy-to-navigate segments. Explore *Career Ideas for Teens* in...

- Agriculture, Food, and Natural Resources
- Architecture and Construction
- Arts and Communications
- Business, Management, and Administration
- Education and Training
- Finance
- Government and Public Service
- Health Science
- Hospitality and Tourism
- Human Services
- Information Technology
- Law and Public Safety
- Manufacturing
- Marketing
- Science, Technology, Engineering, and Math
- Transportation, Distribution, and Logistics

think about what you really want to do. Better yet, stick around until you get a sense of the skills, interests, ambitions, and values you already possess that can take you places in the real world.

Sure, this first step can be a doozy. It's also one that many people miss. Just talk to the adults in your life about their career choices. Find out how many of them took the time to choose a career based on personal preferences and strengths. Then ask how many of them wish now that they had. You're likely to learn that if they had it to do over again, they would jump at the chance to make well-informed career choices.

SECTION TWO: EXPLORE YOUR OPTIONS

Next, come all the career ideas you'd expect to find in a book called *Career Ideas for Teens*. Each of the 35 careers featured in this section represents possible destinations along a career cluster pathway. With opportunities associated with 16 different career clusters—everything from agriculture and art to transportation and technology—you're sure to find intriguing new ideas to consider. Forget any preconceived notions about what you (or others) think you *should* be and take some time to figure out what you really want to be. Put all the things you discovered about yourself in Section One to good use as you explore the world of work.

SECTION THREE: EXPERIMENT WITH SUCCESS

What would it really be like to be a…whatever it is you want to be? Why wait until it's too late to change your mind to find out? Here's your chance to take career ideas of interest for a test drive. Play around with this one; give that one a try…. It's a no-pressure, no-obligation way to find work you really want to do.

This three-step process is about uncovering potential (yours) and possibilities (career paths). Plunge in, give it some thought, uncover the clues, put the pieces together…whatever it takes to find the way to your very best future!

DISCOVER YOU AT WORK

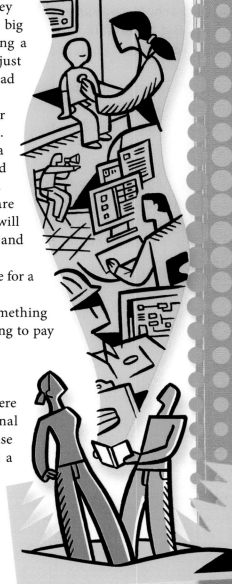

Sometimes people make things harder than they have to be. Like waiting until the night before a big exam to start studying.... Agonizing over asking a special someone to the prom instead of, um, just asking.... Worrying about finishing a project instead of sitting down and doing it....

Figuring out what you want to do with your life can be that way, too. Sure, it is a big decision. And, yes, the choices you make now can have a big impact on the rest of your life. But, there's good news. You don't have to figure everything out now.

Bottom line, every potential employer you are likely to encounter throughout your entire career will want to know two things: "What do you know?" and "What can you do?"

That being the case, what can you do to prepare for a successful career?

Two things: 1) Become a skilled expert in something that you like to do, and 2) find an employer willing to pay you to do it.

Really.

It's that simple...and that complicated.

"Me, Myself, and I" offers a starting point where you can uncover insightful clues about personal interests, skills, values, and ambitions you can use to make sound career decisions. Think through a round of who, what, when, where, how questions in "Me, Myself, and I" about you and then move on to "Hello, World of Work," where you'll discover how to match what you want from work with what specific types of skills employers need from you.

SOME GOOD ADVICE

"If you want an average successful life, it doesn't take much planning. Just stay out of trouble, go to school, and apply for jobs you might like. But if you want something extraordinary, you have two choices:

1. Become the best at one specific thing.
2. Become very good (top 25 percent) at two or more things.

The first strategy is difficult to the point of near impossibility. Few people will ever play in the NBA or make a platinum album. I don't recommend anyone even try.

The second strategy is fairly easy. Everyone has at least a few areas in which they could be in the top 25 percent with some effort. In my case, I can draw better than most people can, but I'm hardly an artist. And I'm not any funnier than the average standup comedian who never makes it big, but I'm funnier than most people. The magic is that few people can draw well and write jokes. It's the combination of the two that makes what I do so rare. And when you add in my business background, suddenly I had a topic that few cartoonists could hope to understand without living it."

—*Scott Adams,*
creator of the Dilbert *comic strip*

Me, Myself, and I

Why do I need to learn all this stuff? Chances are that at some point in the dozen or so years you have already spent in school you have asked this question a time or two. Come on. What can quadratic polynomials and the periodic table of elements possibly have to do with the rest of your life?

Among other things, your education is supposed to get you ready to succeed in the real world. Yes, all those grammar rules and mathematical mysteries will someday come in handy no matter what you end up doing. Nevertheless, more than all the facts and figures you've absorbed, the plan all along—from kindergarten to graduation—has been to make sure you learn how to learn.

If you know how to learn, you'll know how to seek out and acquire pretty much anything you need or want to know. Get the knowledge, gain the skills, and the resulting expertise is your ticket to a successful career.

As its title suggests, this chapter is all about you—and for a very good reason. Your traits, interests, skills, work style, and values offer important clues you can use to make important decisions about your future—for valid reasons with intention and purpose.

And, speaking of clues...

Think of yourself like a good mystery, but instead of sleuthing out whodunit, focus on collecting evidence about you. By the time you have completed the following six activities, you'll be ready to encounter the world of work on your own terms.

Discover #1: WHO Am I?
Discover #2: WHAT Do I Like to Do?
Discover #3: WHERE Does My Work Style Fit Best?
Discover #4: WHY Do My Work Values Matter?
Discover #5: HOW Ready Am I for the 21st-Century Workplace?
Discover #6: "Me" Résumé

ON SUCCESS
If you don't know what you want, how will you know when you get it?

ON LIFE DIRECTION
If you don't know where you are going, how will you know when you get there?

DISCOVER #1: WHO AM I?

Make a grid with three columns and six rows on a blank sheet of paper. Number each row from one to six.

- In the first row, write the three best words you'd use to describe yourself.
- In the second row, ask a good friend what three words they'd use to describe you.
- In the third row, ask a favorite teacher for three words that she thinks best describe you.
  - In the fourth row, ask a coach, club adviser, youth leader, or other adult mentor to use three words to describe you.
  - In the fifth row, ask a sibling or other young relative to take a crack at describing you.
  - In the sixth row, ask a parent or trusted adult relative for three descriptive words about you.

You			
Friend			
Teacher			
Coach or mentor			
Sibling or young relative			
Parent or adult relative			

Discovery #1: I Am...

Look for common themes in the way that others see you and compare them with the way you see yourself. Include the words used most often to describe you to write an official, ready-for-*Merriam-Webster's-Dictionary* definition of you.

_____

_____

_____

DISCOVER #2: WHAT DO I LIKE TO DO?

Think fast! Use a blank sheet of paper to complete the following statements with the first answers that come to mind.

1 I like to _____ , _____ ,

and _____ .

2 I am really good at _____ ,

_____ , and _____ .

3 I totally suck at _____ , _____ ,

and _____ .

4 Something I can do for hours without getting bored is

_____ .

5 One thing that absolutely bores me to tears is

_____ .

6 My favorite subjects in school are _____ ,

_____ , and _____ .

7 In my free time, I especially like to _____ ,

_____ , and _____ .

8 Something I'd really like to learn how to do is

_____ .

9 Other people compliment me most often about

_____ .

Discovery #2: I Like...

Use your responses to the prompts above to create a list of your three top interests. See if you can identify off the top of your head at least three careers with a direct connection to each interest.

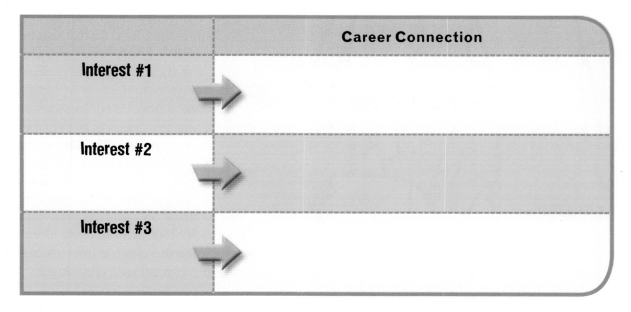

	Career Connection
Interest #1	
Interest #2	
Interest #3	

DISCOVER #3: WHERE DOES MY WORK STYLE FIT BEST?

It is your first day on the job and it's time for lunch. Walking into the employee cafeteria, you discover six tables. There is a big welcome sign instructing new employees to find the table that best matches his or her style. You quickly conclude that they aren't talking about preppy or retro fashions and start looking for other things you share in common. Read the following descriptions and choose the table where you fit in best.

Table 1: The Doers

These people do what it takes to get the job done, whether it involves building, fixing, or growing things, training people, or playing sports. They are practical, hands-on problem solvers who especially enjoy the great outdoors. Forget the paperwork and keep the human interaction to a minimum—these people would rather do something than talk about it. Among the colleagues seated at this table are an aerospace engineer, architect, carpenter, chef, civil engineer, park ranger, and police officer.

Table 2: The Thinkers

These people have never met a fact they didn't like. With a preference for tasks that require mental acuity over physical activity, you're likely to encounter as many laptops as lunchboxes here. Well known for insatiable curiosity, be prepared to answer lots of questions, discuss off-the-wall-subjects, and take a shot at the latest brainteaser circulating around the table. Feel free to strike up a conversation with your pick of an archaeologist, chiropractor, computer programmer, electrician, ecologist, psychologist, or zoologist.

ORGANIZER

HELPER

THINKER

DOER

CREATOR

PERSUADER

TAKE A SEAT!

A few things you'll want to know about these "lunch tables":

1. Each "table" represents one of the widely used Holland codes. This classification system was developed by psychologist Dr. John Holland as a way to link six distinct personality types to career choices and work success. The official work personality types include:
   - Doers = Realistic (R)
   - Thinkers = Investigative (I)
   - Creators = Artistic (A)
   - Helpers = Social (S)
   - Persuaders = Enterprising (E)
   - Organizers = Conventional (C)

2. There is no "best" work personality. It takes all kinds to keep the world working. When everything is in balance, there's a job for every person and a person for every job.
3. You, like most people, are probably a unique combination of more than one personality type: a little of this, a lot of that. That's what makes people interesting.

You can go online, plug in your work personality codes, and find lists of interest-related career options at http://online.onetcenter.org/find/descriptor/browse/Interests.

Table 3: The Creators

Here you'll find the artsy, free-spirit types—those drawn to words, art, and other forms of creative self-expression. Rules and structure tend to box in these out-of-the-box thinkers. Doing their own thing

WHAT'S YOUR STYLE?

ARE YOU A DOER?

Are you:
- Independent?
- Reserved?
- Practical?
- Mechanical?
- Athletic?
- Persistent?

Do you like:
- Building things?
- Training animals?
- Playing sports?
- Fixing things?
- Gardening?
- Hunting?
- Fishing?

ARE YOU A THINKER?

Are you:
- Logical?
- Independent?
- Analytical?
- Observant?
- Inquisitive?

Do you like:
- Exploring new subjects?
- Doing puzzles?
- Messing around with computers?
- Solving mysteries?
- Keeping up with the latest news and world events?
- Tackling new challenges?

ARE YOU A CREATOR?

Are you:
- Imaginative?
- Intuitive?
- Expressive?
- Emotional?
- Creative?
- Independent?

Do you like:
- Drawing?
- Painting?
- Playing an instrument?
- Visiting museums?
- Acting?
- Designing clothes ?
- Decorating spaces?
- Reading?
- Traveling?
- Writing?

ARE YOU A HELPER?

Are you:

- Friendly?
- Outgoing?
- Empathic?
- Persuasive?
- Idealistic?
- Generous?

Do you like:

- Joining clubs?
- Playing team sports?
- Caring for children?
- Going to parties?
- Meeting new people?

ARE YOU A PERSUADER?

Are you:

- Assertive?
- Self-confident?
- Ambitious?
- Extroverted?
- Optimistic?
- Adventurous?

Do you like:

- Organizing parties and other events?
- Selling things?
- Promoting ideas?
- Giving speeches?
- Starting businesses?

ARE YOU AN ORGANIZER?

Are you:

- Well-organized?
- Accurate?
- Practical?
- Persistent?
- Conscientious?
- Ambitious?

Do you like:

- Working with numbers?
- Collecting or organizing things?
- Proofreading?
- Keeping records?
- Keeping yourself and others on track?

MY WORK STYLE(S) IS...

- ❑ Doer (Realistic)
- ❑ Thinker (Investigative)
- ❑ Creator (Artistic)
- ❑ Helper (Social)
- ❑ Persuader (Enterprising)
- ❑ Organizer (Conventional)

is what they do best. Among your potential lunch companions are an actor, cartoon animator, choreographer, drama teacher, fashion designer, graphic designer, interior designer, journalist, and writer.

Table 4: Helpers

Good luck trying to get a word in edgewise at this table. Helpers are "people" people: always ready for a good chat or to lend a helping hand. Communicating with others trumps working with objects, machines, or data. They are all about serving people, promoting learning, and making the world a better place. Sit down and get acquainted with an arbitrator, art therapist, childcare worker, coach, counselor, cruise director, fitness trainer, registered nurse, and teacher.

Table 5: The Persuaders

While helpers focus on helping people, persuaders are natural leaders or managers—especially adept at getting people to do what they want them to do. These people are more about action than analysis, equally comfortable with taking risks and responsibility. Entrepreneurs at heart, they like to make things happen. Sit down and find your place among peers such as an advertising executive, criminal investigator, lawyer, lobbyist, school principal, stockbroker, and urban planner.

Table 6: The Organizers

Organizers are people you can count on to cross their t's and dot their i's. In other words, no detail escapes their careful attention. Most comfortable doing things "by the book," organizers thrive on routine and structure. A penchant for following instructions and respecting authority gives these types something of a squeaky-clean reputation. Make yourself comfortable and enjoy a nice break with an accountant, actuary, air traffic controller, chief financial officer, economist, mathematician, and paralegal.

DISCOVER #4: WHY DO MY WORK VALUES MATTER?

There's another thing to consider before evaluating all of the clues you've gathered. According to O*Net OnLine, America's primary source of occupational information, six types of values are commonly associated with workplace satisfaction: achievement, independence, recognition, relationships, support, and working conditions. Read each of the following statements and put an X in the box preceding those that are important to you.

In considering my future career, it matters most that

❑   1.   I make use of my abilities.

❑   2.   I can try out my own ideas.

❑   3.   I can give directions and instructions to others.

❑   4.   I would never be pressured to do things that go against my sense of right and wrong.

❑   5.   I would be treated fairly by the company.

❑   6.   The job would provide for steady employment.

❑   7.   I enjoy the satisfaction of a job well done.

❑   8.   I can make decisions on my own.

❑   9.   I could receive recognition for the work I do.

❑   10.   I could do things for other people.

❑   11.   I have supervisors who would support their workers with management.

❑   12.   My pay would compare well with that of other workers.

❑   13.   What I do matters.

❑   14.   I can work with little supervision.

❑   15.   The job would provide an opportunity for advancement.

❑   16.   My coworkers would be easy to get along with.

❑   17.   I have supervisors who train their workers well.

❑   18.   The job would have good working conditions.

❑ **19.** I find a sense of accomplishment in my work.

❑ **20.** I have some flexibility in when and how I do my work.

❑ **21.** My work efforts are appreciated.

❑ **22.** I have the opportunity to work with all kinds of people.

❑ **23.** My work expectations are clearly defined and necessary resources are provided.

❑ **24.** I could do something different every day.

Tally up your results here.

Achievement	Independence	Recognition
❑ 1	❑ 2	❑ 3
❑ 7	❑ 8	❑ 9
❑ 13	❑ 14	❑ 15
❑ 19	❑ 20	❑ 21
Total	**Total**	**Total**
Relationships	**Support**	**Working Conditions**
❑ 4	❑ 5	❑ 6
❑ 10	❑ 11	❑ 12
❑ 16	❑ 17	❑ 18
❑ 22	❑ 23	❑ 24
Total	**Total**	**Total**

Your Work Values at Work

Once you've clued yourself in to what's important to you in a career, you need to connect those values to actual jobs.

Achievement: If Achievement is your highest work value, look for jobs that let you use your best abilities. Look for work where you can see the results of your efforts. Explore jobs where you can get a genuine sense of accomplishment.

Independence: If Independence is your highest work value, look for jobs where employers let you do things on your own initiative. Explore work where you can make decisions on your own.

Recognition: If Recognition is your highest work value, explore jobs that come with good possibilities for advancement. Look for work with prestige or with the potential for leadership.

Relationships: If Relationships are your highest work value, look for jobs where your coworkers are friendly. Look for work that lets you be of service to others. Explore jobs that do not make you do anything that goes against your sense of right and wrong.

Support: If Support is your highest work value, look for jobs where the company stands behind its workers and where supervision is handled in supportive ways. Explore work in companies with a reputation for competent, considerate, and fair management.

Working Conditions: If Working Conditions are your highest work value, consider pay, job security, and good working conditions when looking at jobs. Look for work that suits your work style. Some people like to be busy all the time, or work alone, or have many different things to do.

Discovery #4: My Work Values Include
- ❏ Achievement
- ❏ Independence
- ❏ Recognition
- ❏ Relationships
- ❏ Support
- ❏ Working Conditions

DISCOVER #5: HOW READY AM I FOR THE 21ST-CENTURY WORKPLACE?

Are you ready for the 21st-century workforce? Some of America's most prominent employers and educators want to make sure. They put their heads together and came up with a list of essential skills, called 21st-century skills, which they recommend you bring to your first big job.

Some of these skills you've been busy acquiring without even knowing it. For instance, every time you go online to play games or do a little social networking you are cultivating important technology skills. Other skills will take some work. You can find an official description of these skills at http://www.p21.org. In the meantime, you can do a very informal assessment of your workplace skills using this 21st-century skills meter.

21st-CENTURY SKILLS METER

On the following scales, 1 represents total cluelessness, 10 represents impressive competency of the straight-A variety, and 2–9 represent varying degrees in between

How would you describe your mastery of the following subject:

	1	2	3	4	5	6	7	8	9	10
English, reading, and language arts?										
Foreign language?										
Arts?										
Mathematics?										
Economics?										
Science?										
Geography?										
History?										
Government and civics?										

How would you rate your current knowledge about:

	1	2	3	4	5	6	7	8	9	10
Global issues?										
Other cultures, religions, and lifestyles?										
Managing your personal finances?										
Understanding the world of work?										
Using entrepreneurial skills to enhance workplace productivity and career options?										

(continues)

21st-CENTURY SKILLS METER *(continued)*	1	2	3	4	5	6	7	8	9	10
Local and national political events?										
Being part of the democratic process?										
Making good choices about your health and wellness?										
How good are you at:										
Making good decisions using sound judgment based on careful evaluation of evidence and ideas?										
Solving problems using both common sense and innovative ideas?										
Communicating thoughts and ideas verbally?										
Communicating thoughts and ideas in writing?										
Using various types of media and technology to inform, instruct, motivate, and/or persuade?										
Collaborating with others and working as a team?										

21st-CENTURY SKILLS METER

	1	2	3	4	5	6	7	8	9	10
Finding information in a wide variety of ways that includes books, newspapers, the Internet, etc.?										
Quickly learning how to use new technologies such as smart phones and online games?										
Getting used to new situations and finding the middle ground in disagreements?										
Thinking "out of the box" in creative and innovative ways?										
Understanding world issues and global cultures?										
Finding ways to protect and sustain the earth's environment?										

Discovery #5: I Am Getting Ready for the 21st-Century Workforce...

Use the two columns below to list skills you are already actively cultivating (those you scored 6 or higher) and those you need to take steps to pursue (those you scored 5 or lower).

In Progress	In Pursuit

DISCOVER #6: "ME" RÉSUMÉ

Eventually you will need to put together a job-hunting résumé that presents in a concise and compelling way all the reasons an employer should hire you. But, you aren't looking for a job right now. You are looking for a future.

It just so happens that creating a résumé with a twist offers a great way to make sense of all the fascinating facts you've just discovered about yourself. It also offers the double-whammy benefit of practicing your résumé-writing skills. So use the following format to create a "me" résumé summarizing what you've just learned about yourself in a professional way.

NAME
I am...
(* Put the definition of you here)
I like...
(* Key interests)
I work best...
(* Work style)
I most value...
(* Work values)
I am getting ready for the 21st-century workforce...
(* 21st-century skills already acquired and in process)

Hello, World of Work

Pop quiz!

What are the two things necessary for finding a successful career?

Hint #1: You started thinking about some interesting options for one of these "ingredients" in "Me, Myself, and I."

Hint #2: You are about to find out how to find the second ingredient in "Hello, World of Work."

Give yourself an A+ if your answer is anything like

1 Become an expert in something that you like to do, and
2 Find an employer who is willing to pay you to do it.

Finding a career you want to pursue is only half the challenge. The flipside involves finding out what the world of work wants from you. Keep the clues you discovered about yourself in the "Me, Myself, and I" section in the back of your mind as the focus shifts from self-discovery to work-discovery.

It's a big world out there—finding a path where you can get where you want to go is the next order of business.

DISCOVER #7: WHERE CAN MY INTERESTS AND SKILLS TAKE ME?

First, a confession: The following interest inventory is intended for use as an informal career exploration tool. It makes no claims of scientific validity or statistical reliability.

It was inspired by (and used with permission of) the Career Clusters Interest Survey developed by the States' Career Clusters Initiative, and the Oklahoma Department of Career and Technology Education. It includes significant revisions, however, that are meant to offer an age-appropriate, self-discovery tool to teens like you.

Your school guidance office can provide information about formal assessment and aptitude resources you may want to use at some point. In the meantime, use this informal interest inventory to start your exploration process and to make the connection between you and the world of work.

Following are eight different lists representing diverse interests that range from childhood play preferences to save-the-world ambitions. Each type of interest offers unique insight about career paths that may take you where you want to go in life.

Read each question and choose the response(s) that are most true for you.

When you were a little kid, what was your favorite thing to do?

❑   **1.**   Play outside, explore nature, plan big adventures.

❑   **2.**   Build things with Lego's, Lincoln logs, or other construction sets.

❑   **3.**   Put on plays to entertain your family and friends.

❑   **4.**   Run a lemonade stand.

❑   **5.**   Pretend you were a teacher and play school.

❑   **6.**   Play storekeeper and run the cash register with phony money.

❑   **7.**   Pretend you were president of the United States or boss of the world.

❑   **8.**   Play doctor and nurse your stuffed animals and siblings back to health.

❑   **9.**   Get your friends and neighbors together for backyard games, obstacle courses, or secret clubs.

❑   **10.**   Take care of stray animals, play with pets, pet-sit for neighbors.

❑   **11.**   Play Nintendo, Game Boy, or other kinds of video games.

❑   **12.**   Take turns being the "bad guy" in cops and robbers or use a spy kit to collect fingerprints and other clues.

❑   **13.**   Build model planes or cars or come up with new inventions.

❑   **14.**   Do arts and crafts.

☐ 15. Concoct new formulas with a junior chemistry set.

☐ 16. Play with cars, trucks, and trains, and build roads and bridges.

Which of the following lists of subjects would you most like to study?

☐ 1. Biology, botany, chemistry, ecology, horticulture, zoology.

☐ 2. Art, computer-aided design, drafting, construction trades, geometry.

☐ 3. Art, broadcasting, creative writing, graphic design, journalism, music, theater arts.

☐ 4. Accounting, business, cooperative education, economics, information technology.

☐ 5. Child development, family and consumer studies, psychology, social studies, sociology.

☐ 6. Accounting, business law, business math, economics, personal finance.

☐ 7. Civics and government, current events, debate, foreign language, history, philosophy.

☐ 8. Biology, chemistry, health, math, occupational health, language arts.

☐ 9. Culinary arts, food service, foreign language, geography, language arts, speech.

☐ 10. Anthropology, family and consumer science, foreign language, language arts, psychology, sociology.

☐ 11. Communication, computer applications, graphic design, math, science, technology education.

☐ 12. First aid, forensic science, government, health, history, language arts, law enforcement, psychology.

☐ 13. Chemistry, geometry, language arts, physics, shop, trades.

14. Business education, computer applications, distributive education, economics, language arts, marketing.

15. Computer-aided design, computer networking, drafting, electronics, engineering, math, science.

16. Economics, foreign language, math, physical science, trade and industry.

Which type of afterschool club or activity are you more likely to join?

1. 4-H, Future Farmers of America (FFA), community gardening.

2. Habitat for Humanity, construction club, trade apprenticeship.

3. Dance, drama, chorus, marching band, newspaper staff, yearbook staff.

4. Future Business Leaders of America (FBLA), Junior Achievement.

5. National Honor Society, peer-to-peer mentor, tutor.

6. Stock Market Game, investment club.

7. Student government, debate team.

8. Sports trainer, Health Occupations Students of America (HOSA), Red Cross volunteer.

9. Culture Club, International Club, Model United Nations Club.

10. Beta Club; Key Club; Family, Career and Community Leaders of America (FCCLA).

11. High-Tech Club, Technology Student Association (TSA), Video Gamers Club.

12. Law Enforcement Explorer Post.

13. Odyssey of the Mind, SkillsUSA/Vocational Industrial Clubs of America (VICA).

14. Distributive Education Clubs of America (DECA) Marketing Club, junior fashion advisory board.

- ❏ 15. Junior Engineering Technical Society (JETS), math club, National High School Science Bowl, science club.
- ❏ 16. Environmental awareness clubs, National High School Solar Car Race.

Which of the following weekend activities would you most enjoy doing?

- ❏ 1. Fishing, hunting, or hiking.
- ❏ 2. Building a house for a needy family with Habitat for Humanity.
- ❏ 3. Going to a concert or to see the latest movie.
- ❏ 4. Getting a part-time job.
- ❏ 5. Volunteering at the library or reading stories to children at a homeless shelter.
- ❏ 6. Staying up all night playing Monopoly with friends.
- ❏ 7. Working on a favorite political candidate's election campaign.
- ❏ 8. Hosting a big birthday bash for a friend.
- ❏ 9. Helping out at the local Ronald McDonald House or children's hospital.
- ❏ 10. Taking a Red Cross first aid course or disaster-relief course.
- ❏ 11. Playing a new video game or setting up a new home page for social networking.
- ❏ 12. Watching all your favorite cop shows on TV.
- ❏ 13. Giving your room an eco-makeover.
- ❏ 14. Making posters to celebrate homecoming or a big school event.
- ❏ 15. Competing in a local science fair.
- ❏ 16. Building a soapbox derby car to race with friends.

Which of the following group of words best describes you?

- ❑ **1.** Adventurous, eco-friendly, outdoorsy, physically active.
- ❑ **2.** Artistic, curious, detail oriented, patient, persistent, visual thinker.
- ❑ **3.** Creative, determined, dramatic, imaginative, talkative, tenacious.
- ❑ **4.** Logical, natural leader, practical, organized, responsible, tactful.
- ❑ **5.** Attentive, decisive, friendly, helpful, innovative, inquisitive.
- ❑ **6.** Efficient, good with numbers, logical, methodical, orderly, self-confident, trustworthy.
- ❑ **7.** Articulate, competitive, organized, persuasive, problem-solver, service minded.
- ❑ **8.** Attentive, careful, caring, compassionate, conscientious, patient, task oriented.
- ❑ **9.** Adventurous, easygoing, fun loving, outgoing, self-motivated, tactful.
- ❑ **10.** Accepting, attentive, articulate, intuitive, logical, sensible, thrifty.
- ❑ **11.** Accurate, analytical, detail oriented, focused, logical, persistent, precise, technology whiz.
- ❑ **12.** Adventurous, community minded, courageous, dependable, decisive, fair, optimistic.
- ❑ **13.** Active, coordinated, inquisitive, observant, practical, steady.
- ❑ **14.** Competitive, creative, enthusiastic, persuasive, self-motivated.
- ❑ **15.** Curious about how things work, detail oriented, inquisitive, objective, mechanically inclined, observant.
- ❑ **16.** Coordinated, mechanical, multitasker, observant, prepared, realistic.

If you could do only one thing to make the world a better place, which of the following would you do?

❑   **1.**   Eliminate hunger everywhere.

❑   **2.**   Create sustainable, eco-friendly environments.

❑   **3.**   Keep the world entertained and informed.

❑   **4.**   Provide meaningful jobs and fair trade opportunities for everyone.

❑   **5.**   Teach the world to read so that no one is limited by a lack of education.

❑   **6.**   Keep national and global financial systems on track.

❑   **7.**   Promote world peace and stable governments for all.

❑   **8.**   Provide access to high-quality health care services for everyone.

❑   **9.**   Bridge cultural differences through communication and collaboration.

❑   **10.**   Help people in need get back on their feet.

❑   **11.**   Use technology to solve the world's most pressing problems.

❑   **12.**   Make the world a safer place where justice prevails.

❑   **13.**   Discover a new innovation on par with Edison's invention of electricity that has the potential to improve the quality of life for all mankind.

❑   **14.**   Get the word out about a favorite issue or cause.

❑   **15.**   Find a cure for cancer, AIDS, or other life-threatening disease.

❑   **16.**   Develop more efficient ways to get people and things where they need to go.

Which of the following lists of career options intrigues you most?

- ❏ 1. Agricultural economist, botanist, food broker, food scientist, forester, geologist, hydrologist, nutritionist, recycler, wastewater manager.
- ❏ 2. Civil engineer, demolition technician, energy-efficient builder, heavy-equipment operator, landscape architect, urban planner.
- ❏ 3. Actor, blogger, commercial artist, digital media specialist, museum curator, social medial consultant, stage manager, writer.
- ❏ 4. Advertising account executive, brand manager, budget analyst, chief executive officer, dispatcher, e-commerce analyst, green entrepreneur, international businessperson, purchasing agent.
- ❏ 5. Animal trainer, coach, college professor, corporate trainer, guidance counselor, principal, speech pathologist, textbook publisher.
- ❏ 6. Accountant, banker, chief financial officer, economist, fraud investigator, investment adviser, property manager, stock broker, wealth manager.
- ❏ 7. Bank examiner, city planner, customs agent, federal special agent, intelligence analyst, politician, private investigator.
- ❏ 8. Art therapist, audiologist, chiropractor, dentist, massage therapist, pharmacist, surgeon, veterinarian.
- ❏ 9. Banquet manager, chef, cruise ship captain, exhibit designer, golf pro, resort manager, theme park designer, tour guide, wedding planner.
- ❏ 10. Career coach, child care director, elder care center manager, hairstylist, personal trainer, psychologist, religious leader, teacher, victim advocate.

☐   **11.** Artificial intelligence scientist, chief information officer, computer forensics investigator, database modeler, e-commerce entrepreneur, Webmaster.

☐   **12.** Animal control officer, coroner, detective, emergency medical technician, firefighter, lawyer, park ranger, warden, wildlife conservation officer.

☐   **13.** Chemical engineer, hybrid car designer, industrial designer, logistician, millwright, nanotechnologist, robotics technologist, traffic engineer, welder.

☐   **14.** Art designer, business development manager, copywriter, creative director, graphic designer, market researcher, media buyer, new media specialist, retail store manager, social media consultant.

☐   **15.** Aeronautical engineer, anthropologist, chemist, ecologist, telecommunications engineer, mathematician, oceanographer, zoologist.

☐   **16.** Air traffic controller, cargo inspector, flight attendant, logistics planner, pilot, railroad engineer, surveyor, truck driver.

Which of the following types of work environments would you most like to work in?

☐   **1.** Farm, food processing plant, food science laboratory, forest, garden center, greenhouse, national park, recycling center.

☐   **2.** Construction site, commercial facilities, government agency, corporate office, private firm, residential properties.

☐   **3.** Independent, creative business, museum, news agency, publishing company, studio, theater.

☐   **4.** Business planning office, corporate headquarters, government agency, international business center.

- [ ] 5. College counseling center, elementary school, high school, middle school, museum, preschool, school district office.
- [ ] 6. Accounting firm, bank, brokerage firm, corporate office, insurance company, stock market.
- [ ] 7. Business development office, chamber of commerce, city/county/state/federal government agency; courthouse; law firm.
- [ ] 8. Dental office, hospital, medical research center, pharmacy, physician's office, surgical complex, urgent care center, veterinary clinic.
- [ ] 9. Airport, amusement park, hotel, public park, resort, restaurant, sports center, travel agency, zoo.
- [ ] 10. Employment agency, consumer credit bureau, elder care center, fitness center, mental health care center, real estate office, school, spa.
- [ ] 11. Corporation, information technology company, new media development center, research and development laboratory, small business.
- [ ] 12. Courthouse, prison, fire station, government agency, law firm, national park, police station.
- [ ] 13. Manufacturing plant, design firm, engineering company, production facility, research and development laboratory.
- [ ] 14. Advertising agency, independent creative business, corporate marketing department, retail store, new media development center.
- [ ] 15. Science laboratory, engineering firm, information technology company, research and development center.
- [ ] 16. Airport, marina, mass transit authority, railroad, shipping port, subway system, transportation center.

Go back through your answers and record how many of each of the following numbers you have marked.

1s	2s	3s	4s	5s	6s	7s	8s
9s	10s	11s	12s	13s	14s	15s	16s

Discovery #7: My Interests and Skills...

What do your answers say about your personal preferences, natural inclinations, and ambitions? In what ways can you use these clues to better inform your career choices? What general direction are your skills and interests pointing toward? Describe below.

_____

_____

_____

_____

_____

_____

DISCOVER #8: WHICH CAREER PATH IS RIGHT FOR ME?

If you had more...	Consider this career cluster...	To explore careers that involve...
1s	Agriculture, Food, and Natural Resources	Producing, processing, marketing, distributing, financing, and developing agricultural commodities and resources including food, fiber, wood products, natural resources, horticulture, and other plant and animal products and resources.
2s	Architecture and Construction	Designing, planning, managing, building, and maintaining the built environment.
3s	Arts, A/V Technology, and Communications	Designing, producing, exhibiting, performing, writing, and publishing multimedia content including visual and performing arts and design, journalism, and entertainment services.
4s	Business, Management, and Administration	Planning, organizing, directing, and evaluating business functions essential to efficient and productive business operations.
5s	Education and Training	Planning, managing, and providing education and training services, and related learning support services.
6s	Finance	Planning services for financial and investment planning, banking, insurance, and business financial management.
7s	Government and Public Service	Governing, planning, regulating, managing, and administering governmental functions at the local, state, and federal levels.
8s	Health Science	Planning, managing, and providing therapeutic services, diagnostic services, health informatics, support services, and biotechnology research and development.

(continues)

(continued)

If you had more...	Consider this career cluster...	To explore careers that involve...
9s	Hospitality and Tourism	Managing, marketing, and operating restaurants and other food services, lodging, attractions, recreation events, and travel-related services.
10s	Human Services	Preparing individuals for employment in career pathways that relate to families and human needs.
11s	Information Technology	Designing, developing, supporting, and managing hardware, software, multimedia, and systems integration services.
12s	Law, Public Safety, Corrections, and Security	Planning, managing, and providing legal, public safety, protective services, and homeland security, including professional and technical support services.
13s	Manufacturing	Planning, managing, and performing the processing of materials into intermediate or final products and related professional and technical support activities.
14s	Marketing	Planning, managing, and performing marketing activities to reach organizational objectives.
15s	Science, Technology, Engineering, and Mathematics	Planning, managing, and providing scientific research and professional and technical services including laboratory and testing services, and research and development services.
16s	Transportation, Distribution, and Logistics	Planning, managing, and moving of people, materials, and goods by road, pipeline, air, rail, and water, and related professional and technical support services.

Gratefully adapted and used with permission from the States' Career Clusters Initiative.

Discovery #8: My Career Path

With all scores tallied and all interests considered, where should you begin exploring your future career? List the three career clusters you most want to explore here:

1 _____

2 _____

3 _____

As you can probably guess, each title in the *Career Ideas for Teens* series is based on one of the career clusters described above. For the most effective career exploration process, start with the title most in sync with both your assessment results and your gut instincts about what you want to do with your life.

No matter which title you choose, be prepared to encounter exciting opportunities you've never considered—maybe even some you've never heard of before. You may find that your interests, skills, and ambitions lead you to a specific career idea that inspires your immediate plans for the future. On the other hand, those same interests, skills, and ambitions may simply point you toward a particular pathway or industry segment such as agriculture or education. That's just fine, too. Time, experience, opportunities—and the "Experiment with Success" activities you'll encounter in Section Three—will eventually converge to get you right where you want to be.

YOU ARE HERE

If you scored high in and are especially curious about...	Start exploring career options in Section Two of...
Agriculture, Food, and Natural Resources	*Career Ideas for Teens in Agriculture, Food, and Natural Resources*
Architecture and Construction	*Career Ideas for Teens in Architecture and Construction, Second Edition*
Arts, A/V Technology, and Communications	*Career Ideas for Teens in the Arts and Communications, Second Edition*
Business, Management, and Administration	*Career Ideas for Teens in Business, Management, and Administration*
Education and Training	*Career Ideas for Teens in Education and Training, Second Edition*
Finance	*Career Ideas for Teens in Finance*
Government and Public Service	*Career Ideas for Teens in Government and Public Service, Second Edition*
Health Science	*Career Ideas for Teens in Health Science, Second Edition*
Hospitality and Tourism	*Career Ideas for Teens in Hospitality and Tourism*
Human Services	*Career Ideas for Teens in Human Services*
Information Technology	*Career Ideas for Teens in Information Technology, Second Edition*
Law, Public Safety, Corrections, and Security	*Career Ideas for Teens in Law and Public Safety, Second Edition*
Manufacturing	*Career Ideas for Teens in Manufacturing, Second Edition*
Marketing	*Career Ideas for Teens in Marketing*
Science, Technology, Engineering, and Mathematics	*Career Ideas for Teens in Science, Technology, Engineering, and Math*
Transportation, Distribution, and Logistics	*Career Ideas for Teens in Transportation, Distribution, and Logistics*

DISCOVER #9: CAREER RÉSUMÉ

In "Me, Myself, and I," you summarized all your discoveries in a "me" résumé. This time, shift the focus to create a career résumé that describes what you currently consider a "dream job." Use a blend of your own wants and opportunities you'd expect to find along your favorite career path to fill in the categories below.

Career Title _____

_____

Job Description _____

_____

_____

Skills Needed _____

_____

_____

Knowledge Required _____

_____

_____

Work Environment _____

_____

_____

Perks and Benefits _____

_____

_____

MOVING ON

Ready to start exploring career ideas? Section Two is where potential and possibilities meet. As you start exploring options associated with this career path, look for those careers that best match the discoveries you've made about yourself. Make sure any opportunity you decide to pursue matches up with all you've just learned about your ambitions, skills, interests, values, and work style.

EXPLORE YOUR OPTIONS

Yours is the very first generation born wired. Computers, the Internet, and cell phones are as commonplace to you as color televisions were to your parent's generation. As one of the most computer-savvy generations in history, students like you are already using technology in ways your parents never dream about. You use them to research papers, write and edit assignments, download music and keep in constant contact with friends. Unlike your parents, you've probably never had the dubious honor of having to retype an entire paper to correct a couple of typos. No, you've been much too busy mastering the technological wonders of computers, smart phones, and the Internet.

In the workplace, technology has infiltrated virtually every industry and impacts—in one way or another—virtually any profession you can imagine. Everyone from auto mechanics to stockbrokers are finding computers to be an essential tool of their trade. Even though technology has already revolutionized the business world and is *finally* beginning to revolutionize education, the fact of the matter is this: You ain't seen nothing yet! The world has yet to see how far technology can take us. Some experts predict that, while previous generations envisioned and built this technological infrastructure, it will be your generation who actually uses it to solve perplexing world problems. What an exciting prospect!

For those of you with an interest in being part of this dynamic and consistently amazing industry, there are four main pathways to consider. You'll find there is something for just about any skill set—from highly technical to highly creative. The opportunities are truly diverse, with new ones still emerging. Follow these pathways to clues about the best careers for you to pursue. The four information technology pathways include:

PROGRAMMING AND SOFTWARE DEVELOPMENT

Designing, developing, and implementing computer systems, programs, and apps are all part of the programming and software development pathway. Careers in this pathway require knowledge of computer operating systems, programming languages, and software development. Professionals working in this pathway generally stay a step ahead of the crowd when it comes to making the most of the latest cutting-edge technologies.

NETWORK SYSTEMS

Network systems is a high-demand pathway with opportunities available in all types of 21st-century industries and all sizes of businesses. Work in this field involves analysis, planning, implementation, design, installation, information, infrastructure, and maintenance. Technical knowledge, specialized training, and in some cases certification in specific types of network systems provide entry and advancement opportunities in this field.

INFORMATION SUPPORT AND SERVICES

Professionals working in information support and services bridge the gap between human users and technology. Represented in this pathway are the people responsible for tasks like implementing computer systems, installing and customizing software, providing technical assistance, managing information systems, and other tasks related to the high-tech needs of the 21st-century workplace.

INTERACTIVE MEDIA

People who work in interactive media spend their days creating, designing, and producing a wide variety of multimedia products and platforms used in business, social media, entertaining, communications, and marketing. Facebook, Web 2.0, and cloud computing (new technologies that let people work and collaborate from any place at any time, and on any device) are examples of major breakthroughs in this pathway.

As you explore the 35 information technology careers profiled in this book, remember to keep in mind what you've learned about yourself. Consider each option in light of what you know about your interests, strengths, work values, and work personality.

Pay close attention to the job requirements. Does it require good math or writing skills? Will you need to be able to take things apart and visualize how they go back together? If you don't

A NOTE ON WEB SITES
Web sites tend to move around a bit. If you have trouble finding a specific site referred to in the following career profiles, use your favorite search engine to search for a specific Web site or type of information.

have the necessary skills, and don't have a strong desire to acquire them, you probably won't enjoy the job.

For instance, several popular TV shows make forensic investigations look like a fascinating career. And it is—for some people. But when considering whether forensic investigation, or any career for that matter, is right for you, think about the realities of what you'll be working with. In this case we're talking lots of chemistry, anatomy, and physics, and, quite frankly, working with dead people. Give each profession a reality check as to how appropriate it is for you.

Applications Developer

Yummy Tummy, a dessert shop that should exist, if it doesn't already, really needs help. The shop lets customers order custom cakes in any of 10 different serving sizes, from "Just the Two of Us" to "A Sweet Night of 1,000 Stars." Yummy Tummy's bakers are terrific. But they seem to be a little short on math skills, often calculating the ratio of ingredients incorrectly when they adapt a recipe from "basic size" to "custom." The owners and bakers know that if their computer could recalculate each recipe correctly, life at the shop would be a lot sweeter.

When the owners discover that you, a regular customer, specialize in applications development, they immediately seek your advice and you accept the delicious assignment. Early in your career you learned that by following the development model of the basic software development life cycle model (SLDC), your projects run smoothly and your clients are satisfied. So you begin with phase one, gathering the requirements. In addition to talking to the bakers, you interview everyone else in the company to see what they would like from the program. The financial managers, for example, would like the application to calculate the total cost of each cake. Knowing the cost of individual ingredients, they can use the information for more profitable pricing.

GET STARTED NOW!

- In School: Learn as many computer languages as possible, advanced algebra, and calculus.
- After School: Try the free online tutorials for C, C++, Java, or Python.
- Around Town: Keep a journal in which you try to imagine the steps that are involved in some everyday activities, such as mail delivery.

CAREER 411

Search It!
Active Software Professionals Alliance at http://aspalliance.com.

Surf It!
Applications errors can have really bad results. Check out some of the "Worst Software Blunders" at http://code-hacker.wetpaint.com/page/Worst+Software+Blunders.

Read It!
Developer.com at http://www.developer.com and Application Development Trends at http://adtmag.com.

Learn It!
Minimum Education: Bachelor's degree and experience with various computing systems and technologies.

Typical Majors: Computer science, software engineering, or math.

Special Skills: Knowledge of several programming languages, understanding of relational databases, ability to work under deadline pressure, detail oriented, analytic and problem-solving skills, and the ability to listen and communicate well.

Earn It!
The median annual salary is $87,790.
(Source: U.S. Department of Labor)

In phase two, design, you create a detailed plan to fulfill the requirements. Your plan describes how the application will fulfill the requirements, what information will reside in the program (recipes and costs), what information users will input (number of servings), the rules for adapting to different sizes (whether some things, like decorations, will not change with the size of the cake), and the layout of each input and result screen. Your design plans often include a diagram showing how the information will be processed.

Now you are ready for phase three, coding or implementation. You, or the programmers you hire, use a common programming language (such as Java, Python, C, or C++) to code this special program to the predetermined specifications—taking extra care to document everything you (or they) do. Soon, the first (or beta) version of your work is ready. The project, however, is not quite finished yet.

Phase four, testing, is critical to identify the bugs or problem that are bound to show up. Every bug requires a careful review of all the code and corrections, and more testing. If an application will be on a client's Web site, additional testing of security features is needed.

When everything works perfectly, you install the program on Yummy Tummy's computer. You will be back regularly, for updates and maintenance. And maybe to sample a cupcake or two!

Yummy Tummy's assignment was a piece of cake compared to other assignments you have had. Your next job may involve creating an application for education or business purposes, for social networking, or even for a mobile device, but whatever the client needs, you've got an app for that.

Artificial Intelligence Scientist

In movies, computers with artificial intelligence (A.I.) have strong emotions: sometimes loving, but often hostile, violent, and ready to destroy all humans. Actually computers with artificial intelligence are already part of daily life—and none of them are out to get us.

The Hollywood version of artificial intelligence is aware of its own existence, able to reason and solve problems, and has an independent mind, characteristics that define "strong" artificial intelligence. Strong artificial intelligence does exist, but only in books, movies, and our imaginations.

Weak artificial intelligence, which does exist, is not self-aware and cannot think independently. It can, however, manipulate rules and data programmed into it to complete tasks it was created to do. Using that kind of artificial intelligence, a computer can complete a word or phrase as you begin typing it. It may look like rational thinking, but it is only the artificial intelligence and human instructions that were programmed into it.

Scientists use artificial intelligence to create robots and other devices that accomplish traditional jobs in faster or more dependable ways, or work in conditions that are unsafe for humans. A.I.

GET STARTED NOW!

- In School: Study computer programming and advanced math.
- After School: Using online resources, learn as much as you can about Java and C++.
- Around Town: Notice where artificial intelligence is probably being used, and where you think it should be used. For example, does the timing of traffic signals automatically change when traffic is heavier or when emergency vehicles are present?

scientists use advanced mathematics, formal logic, signal analysis, and pattern recognition theory to create algorithms (or sets of instructions). Programmers use those algorithms to write the code that eventually gets the device to do its job.

The scientists who write algorithms that tell computers or robots how to act must thoroughly understand how those actions are normally accomplished. For example, A.I. scientists wanted to design a better prosthetic leg, one that could sense and respond to different floor surfaces or angles. They first had to know everything about how a natural leg works and how a leg interacts with the brain. To develop artificial intelligence for stock market trading, A.I. scientists had to know what factors affect the price of a stock and the impact of different combinations of factors.

Artificial intelligence scientists contribute to video games and 3-D animation, and to military planning, tank design, and language study. In medicine they are creating A.I. applications that could communicate images directly to a patient's brain and help restore sight to the blind. They are improving automotive cruise

control, designing adaptive cruise control that could maintain a safe distance from the cars in front of it, no matter what the speed.

The big news to watch for is about IBM's Watson, an artificial intelligence machine that sets new records in understanding and answering complex questions. Watson is so fast and so precise that it can (and did) compete at *Jeopardy!*, the television game show with extremely complex clues that involve irony, riddles, and subtle meanings. Machines that can perform at that level might have benefits for science, finance, health care, and business that we can only imagine today.

Business Intelligence Analyst

Sarah's Closet, a hip (yet fictional) chain of clothing stores for young women, is having a problem. After being very successful in New England, where it originated, the company began to expand across the country.

Unfortunately what worked in New England didn't always work in other parts of the country. Certain styles sold like hotcakes in some stores, but not at all in others. In some stores customers poured in during the day, while in others the business picked up at night.

Sarah's Closet had a lot of detailed information in its database about the purchasing history for each customer, the sales of each item, and the revenue by day and hour for each location. What they needed was someone who could make sense of it all and help them make better planning decisions.

As a business intelligence analyst you are the perfect person to help Sarah's Closet move forward. You have the technical expertise to understand all of the tools and systems that are available to analyze all their data and to look for trends and correlations.

Equally important, however, are your outstanding communication skills. Your ability to talk to people who represent different

GET STARTED NOW!

- In School: Computer science, math, marketing.
- After School: Volunteer to help out in your school store or sports concession stand and see if you can spot some trends.
- Around Town: Take notice of the different types of strategies local businesses use to attract customers and increase sales.

CAREER 411

Search It!
Strategic and Competitive Intelligence Professionals at http://www.scip.org.

Surf It!
Find out about business intelligence listed by topic and industry at http://www.b-eye-network.com.

Read It!
Read chapters about business intelligence from different types of textbooks at http://businessintelligence.com/extracts.asp.

Learn It!
Minimum Education: Bachelor's degree.

Typical Majors: Computer science, management information systems, or computer engineering.

Special Skills: Technical expertise with business intelligence software and tools, strong interpersonal (listening, written and verbal communication) and presentation skills, good analytical and problem-solving skills, and understanding of business and industry practices.

Earn It!
The median annual salary is $78,160.
(Source: U.S. Department of Labor)

interests within the company, sometimes called the "stakeholders," and get to the heart of what each one needs is critical. Financial managers, for example, might be most interested in profit margins, effects of sales and discounts, and labor costs. The inventory managers might want to better predict how many of each style, size, and color will sell in each store. Store managers might be most concerned with the number of workers they need to hire for each shift, what items are most likely to be top sellers in their stores, and what a reasonable sales goal is for each week.

Your ability to think critically and creatively is also a strong asset at this stage of the process. You know the importance of asking the right questions, and have often been able to get people to look at variables they had not considered. For example, weather may be important in predicting sales, but perhaps the date that school starts or ends has a bigger impact.

Once you know what each group needs to know, you design reports that show information in a way that is clear and easy to read. Remember that many people involved in making Sarah's

Closet successful are not people who have the time or interest to plow though lots and lots of data.

Now that you have helped Sarah's Closet find a way to reach the highest potential at each location, they've asked you to stay on as a consultant. The economy and fashion are always changing, and your models may have to change, too. If all goes well, Sarah's Closet will need you to analyze the data when they want to open a new location or buy out another chain.

Chief Information Officer

Question: Which of these four scenarios could be a problem for a company's chief information officer (CIO)?

1 The CEO (chief executive officer) wants to know why his is the only competitor in the industry not using Facebook or Twitter.
2 It appears that all confidential customer information was copied when someone hacked into the company's computer system.
3 Customer service telephone lines and the online order entry system cannot handle the additional business created by the company's successful new product launch.
4 Twenty employees have contacted the human resources department about offensive e-mails circulating on company computers.

Answer: Every one of these situations is ultimately the responsibility of the chief information officer.

GET STARTED NOW!

- In School: Computer classes, English, writing and public speaking classes.
- After School: Participate in activities that demonstrate self-confidence and leadership. Run for student council, join the debate team, or participate in an acting workshop or an athletic team.
- Around Town: Get experience working with diverse teams, such as supporting a political candidate, volunteering with organizations that provide a service in the community, or creating public awareness of an issue.

The chief information officer is a critical management person, ultimately responsible for everything related to computing and information technology. He or she monitors the organization's infrastructure (computer and communication hardware, software, databases, people, and policies), to be sure it meets the organization's current and future needs, and reviews every replacement or upgrade proposal. When a project is sufficiently necessary, cost effective, efficient, and flexible, the CIO presents it to the executive management team. Their approval often depends on the CIO's ability to explain what the project will contribute and to communicate complex technical equipment and processes in clear, nontechnical ways.

In addition to managing technology resources, the CIO is responsible for all of the people who work in technology areas. He has to foster a spirit of innovation and workforce productivity, maintain effective communications with department managers, and ensure that those managers effectively communicate company goals and policies to all the members of their teams.

The CIO has ultimate responsibility for managing many of the risks that might threaten the organization. The organization needs well-defined strategies to protect its assets from internal and external security threats and to recover from possible business interruptions that can result from natural disasters, power failures, or terrorist attacks. The company must also be able to comply with all business, personnel, financial, and confidentiality requirements.

The world of information technology is a constantly evolving one. The CIO must stay up-to-date on that evolution and how it might affect his organization or industry. Other members of top management depend on the CIO to explain and keep them up to speed on new trends such as cloud computing (in which services and storage are provided over the Internet), and Web 2.0 (which includes social-networking sites, blogs, wikis, and other Web applications that change users from passive viewers of content to active participants).

The chief information officer position is at the top of the technology ladder. A successful CIO is an experienced leader, an excellent negotiator, and an effective communicator, who also understands business, finance, and all aspects of information technology. It is a tough, demanding job, often the culmination of one's years of experience, education, and hard work.

Computer Programmer

Computers can be so powerful that it is difficult for us to conceive of how fast they can process information. The average desktop computer can complete 100 million calculations per second and the fastest computers can do 1,000 trillion calculations per second!

But, "smart" as computers may be, they can't do anything at all until a human provides detailed instructions. Computers follow those instructions, or programs, precisely and without questions, much the way a well-trained dog might obey its trainer's commands. If, for example, you tell a dog to fetch your slippers, he brings you your slippers. Even if you are dressed for the beach, a formal party, or shoveling snow, when you ask for slippers, you get slippers. Like the dog, computers do not think about whether their instructions make sense. And, while a trainer does not have to tell the dog how to find the slippers, a computer programmer must include every tiny step, including "go to the bedroom" and "open the closet door."

GET STARTED NOW!

- In School: Take as many computer language classes as possible, and advanced algebra and calculus.
- After School: If your school does not offer C, C++, Java, or Python, try an online tutorial or look for classes at your local community college.
- Around Town: Check out local not-for-profit organizations and volunteer to help with their computer systems.

CAREER 411

Search It!
Association for Computing Machinery at http://www.acm.org.

Surf It!
See a visual history of programming at http://www.onlineschools.org/blog/programming.

Read It!
Get an introduction to binary code, compliments of computer giant Intel at http://www97.intel.com/en/TheJourneyInside/ExploreTheCurriculum/EC_DigitalInformation/DILesson1.

Learn It!
Minimum Education: Usually a bachelor's degree, associate's degree, or certificate.

Typical Majors: Computer science, mathematics, or information systems or accounting, finance, or other business area with additional programming courses (especially for programming business applications).

Special Skills: Analytical, attentive to detail, able to stick with a task (even when repetitive), willingness and creativity to try again when a task fails.

Earn It!
The median annual salary is $71,380.
(Source: U.S. Department of Labor)

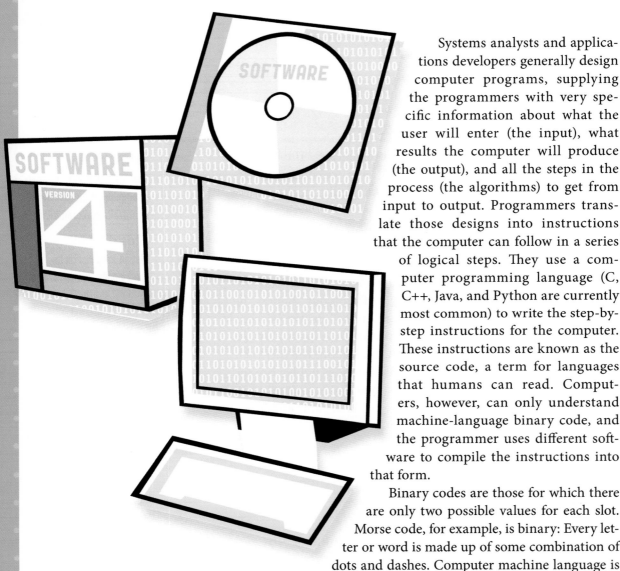

Systems analysts and applications developers generally design computer programs, supplying the programmers with very specific information about what the user will enter (the input), what results the computer will produce (the output), and all the steps in the process (the algorithms) to get from input to output. Programmers translate those designs into instructions that the computer can follow in a series of logical steps. They use a computer programming language (C, C++, Java, and Python are currently most common) to write the step-by-step instructions for the computer. These instructions are known as the source code, a term for languages that humans can read. Computers, however, can only understand machine-language binary code, and the programmer uses different software to compile the instructions into that form.

Binary codes are those for which there are only two possible values for each slot. Morse code, for example, is binary: Every letter or word is made up of some combination of dots and dashes. Computer machine language is also binary: The only possible values are 1 and 0. As you can imagine, binary code is not human-friendly.

Whether a programmer is creating a new program, updating or modifying an existing program, or solving newly discovered problems in an old program, the process always includes testing and fixing and more testing and more fixing. Here's where patience and attention to detail are the programmer's most important assets. Finding a tiny bug (one of those little typos or errors that cause the program to malfunction) can take days, as the programmer goes over every line of code, often multiple times. Today computer programmers have tools that help with programming and debugging to make their work more productive and more interesting.

Programmers have little room for error. Undetected bugs caused the recall of a line of automobiles, the loss of all electrical power in the Northeast, and the disruption of a cell phone system, among other things. It is a field that involves seeing the big picture as well as every tiny detail.

Computer Repair Technician

Sooner or later everyone faces the "repair or replace" dilemma—after all, nothing lives forever. Some decisions are easy: A dead MP3 player is usually replaced; a refrigerator on the fritz is usually (depending on its age) repaired.

When computers have problems, less expensive peripherals tend to get replaced and more expensive components are designated for repair. That's when we call in a computer repair technician who can identify the problem, advise us if we should repair or replace, and then fix the existing component or install a new one. Repair technicians, experts in the workings of computers, do more than fix problems; they also install new equipment and perform maintenance tasks.

If a computer isn't working well, it's because something is malfunctioning in either the hardware or the software. Hardware problems are the result of a physical part of the computer that is no longer functioning well. When that happens to a laptop or desktop computer, the issue can be in the motherboard (the cen-

GET STARTED NOW!

- In School: Electronics, basic computer classes.
- After School: Roll up your sleeves and make some electronics-based gadgets. Find project ideas and instructions at Electronics Project Design at http://www.electronics-project-design.com or at The Electronics Club at http://www.kpsec.freeuk.com/.
- Around Town: Find fix-it shops or television repair shops in your area. See if they will let you spend a day or two observing their repair efforts.

tral printed circuit board that connects all of the parts of a computer together), video cards (that transmit signals from the computer to the monitor), sound cards (that enable us to hear words, music, and sound effects beyond the "beeps" of early computers), hard drives (that store data), or network cards (that allow communication over the network). Repairing hardware can involve a wide range of tools, from the very simple (hand pliers, screwdrivers, and soldering irons) to the very specialized (oscilloscopes and signal generators).

A computer that is running very slowly or a program that is not working at all can indicate a software problem. Things are not always as they seem, though. A printer that no longer prints looks like a hardware problem, but the issue may really be in the software that controls the printer. The "tool kit" for software problems is usually diagnostic software, rather than physical tools for diagnosis.

Mainframe computers, which are large, powerful machines used in industries such as banking, finance, government, and utilities, also experience both hardware and software problems. Computer repair technicians generally specialize in either small, individual machines or large mainframes. For a while the outlook for growth in the mainframe segment of the industry was pessimistic. Although mainframes can run thousands of applications for thousands of users at the same time, they also take up a lot of space and use a lot of energy. The zEnterprise may change that prediction. Launched in 2010 by IBM, it is 40 percent faster than previous mainframes, up to 90 percent more energy efficient, and uses less floor space.

The only safe prediction in the computer industry is that hardware and software will always be changing. Computer repair technicians will always continue their training to keep up with technology and service procedures. The good news? Their jobs are never just "old hat."

Cyber Intelligence Analyst

Have you ever thought about being a spy, saving the world by uncovering secrets and preventing enemy attacks? Did you think you could not qualify because you are not as fearless, athletic, and attractive as the movie spies? Or that you would not be able to uncover and decode enemy secrets at the same time as you engage in romantic encounters, life-threatening fights, and miraculous escapes? No problem. Cyber intelligence analysts are critical to our country's security, and their success depends on technical skills and creative thinking.

Cyber intelligence analysts collect information about hostile countries and organizations. Using this information, they identify, assess, and communicate threats that they discover. Those who specialize in counterintelligence work to protect our information from being collected by others. Others specialize in defensive counterintelligence, making sure that our systems do not have openings through which the hostile factions can enter.

While movie spies always seem to be in beautiful, exotic locations, cyber intelligence analysts are more likely to work in places like Tucson, Arizona, with the artificial intelligence and computer science experts who developed Dark Web, a program that uses data mining and other techniques to identify possible terrorist groups and plans. In the Boston area, computer scientists, statisticians, and linguists at Recorded Future search documents to find

CAREER 411

Search It!
Computer Security News at http://computersecuritynews.us.

Surf It!
Try your hand at cracking code in cryptograms at http://www.greatdaygames.com/games/cryptogram/cryptogram.aspx or http://www.rinkworks.com/brainfood/p/crypts1.shtml.

Read It!
Keep up with the latest government security information at http://www.govinfosecurity.com and at the *Washington Post's* investigation into security agencies at http://projects.washingtonpost.com/top-secret-america/articles/a-hidden-world-growing-beyond-control/.

Learn It!
Minimum Education: Bachelor's degree or extensive experience. Certification as a CISSP (Certified Information System Security Professional) or in Security+.

Typical Majors: Computer science, information systems, or another related field. Some jobs require a bachelor's or master's degree in international relations, foreign or regional studies, or international political science.

(continues)

GET STARTED NOW!

- In School: Computer languages, writing, public speaking, world history, and current events.
- After School: Join your school computer club.
- Around Town: Follow news coverage of cyber attacks and cyber threats to stay current with the field.

(continued)

Special Skills: Knowledge of network and/or operating system security, firewalls, excellent research and analytical skills, excellent writing and communication skills. Salaries are higher for higher security clearance, passing polygraph tests, and fluency in languages of the Middle East, Asia, South Asia, Eastern Europe, or South America.

Earn It!

The median annual salary ranges from $75,000 to $150,000.

(Source: Computerwork.com)

common references or links that might hold clues to terrorists or their plans. Other cyber intelligence agents work in civilian jobs with the Army Intelligence and Security Command, the Office of Naval Intelligence, and government agencies.

Until recently the idea of national security did not call up visions of scientists and mathematicians analyzing Internet posts. The Internet, though, is exactly where the "bad guys" are. In fact terrorists depend on the Internet as much as the rest of us do. They use Web sites, posts, and social networking to spread their ideas, to recruit people to their cause, to share information, and to coordinate attacks. They circulate videos to millions of people to promote terrorist successes and to distribute demonstrations of ways to build bombs.

Surprisingly, many of the most sought-after employees for jobs in cyber intelligence have histories of criminal activity themselves. Government and industry have recognized that those who have

IF YOU WERE. . .

As a cyber intelligence analyst assigned to brief your congressman on what the government is doing about cyber threats, how could you clearly explain the following three issues: what cyber threats are; recent major cyber attacks; government agencies involved in combating cyber threats.

. . . MAKE IT REAL!

Create a large chart for each of the three issues. For each one, present your responses in clear, bullet-point format. HINT: It has been estimated that 1,271 government agencies are working on programs related to counterterrorism, homeland security, and intelligence. List as many of these agencies as you can, writing their main responsibilities next to each one. (You should not include all of them in your briefing.)

now decided to use their considerable skills for more noble purposes can be extremely valuable. After all, "it takes one to know one," and who knows more about unauthorized breaking into files or programs than a successful hacker?

Certified Ethical Hackers who work to break into our own systems (jobs known as penetration testing, intrusion testing, or red teaming) have already identified many potential risks that might have gone unnoticed until real damage occurred.

Certified Ethical Hackers have just one request. They would really appreciate it if the media and the public would refer to those with criminal intent as "crackers," adding dignity to the "hacker" label that they would like to keep for themselves. If these irreplaceable experts are helping our security so much, it doesn't seem like too much to do for them, does it?

Database Administrator

For as long as he could remember, everyone considered Bill's house *the* place to go for dinner. The house wasn't that special, but adults and kids alike were known to salivate just thinking of his mom's cooking. His mom's problem, though, was that she could never find the recipe she planned on making. Vegetarian lasagna, for example, might be filed under vegetables, pasta, Italian dishes, or winter dinners. It was not unusual for her to spend hours searching through too many files and too many cookbooks. What she really needed was a way to organize all her information, so that she could find whatever she wanted quickly and easily. In other words, she needed a database.

Databases are collections of information that are organized by field (categories of information), records (the information in all the fields for one person or place), or files (collections of records). There are several systems that can organize information this way, but the most common type is the relational database management system (RDBMS). An RDBMS sorts data in related tables and allows users to retrieve that data by each field and by linking fields between related records. It can also combine data together from several individual databases and produces data tables based on that combined information. And

GET STARTED NOW!

- In School: Computer programming, statistics.
- After School: If your school does not teach database programs like Microsoft Access, complete an online tutorial on your own.
- Around Town: See how many databases you encounter in everyday life. HINT: Think of your school's staff and student directories and others.

finally, it allows the information to be viewed in many different ways, often defined by the end user.

The job of the database administrator is to work with database management software to determine ways to store, analyze, use, and present data. Among the many methods to accomplish this, one of the most popular is with a computer language called "SQL" (structured query language), which was specially designed for database access. And even though the actual database design is usually performed by database designers or database analysts,

administrators who are familiar with SQL are better able to communicate with everyone on the team and meet the users' goals.

Because the database system must be available 24 hours a day, another aspect of the administrator's job is to monitor the company's hard drives and server and check the error logs. The issue of security is most important. With the increased volume of sensitive information kept in databases, and with so many databases connected to the Internet, it is critical that the information is kept safe and that unauthorized users cannot get into the system.

Problems with a company's database can be extremely costly. Imagine an airline that cannot get into its database for several hours. There go the reservations, the seat assignments, the flight schedules, the credit card payments, the food needs for every flight, as well as the "no fly" list of potential terrorists. Want to give a database administrator a nightmare? Just calculate the cost of the database crashing even for one day!

Database Modeler

Suppose you wanted to help high school students find the colleges that best meet their individual needs. You could create a list for every possible major, and fill each list with all the colleges that offer that major. Then you could do the same for every state, every possible sport, and so on. Eventually you would have a lot of lists. If a student wanted to find schools in Ohio where she could major in art history and join the swim team, she would have to look for schools that appeared on all the relevant lists: Ohio, art history majors, and swim teams. That might take a very long time. On the other hand if all the information were in a database, she could enter all her search terms and easily get her answers.

A database should make it possible for users to get the answer to any question they might ask. The college database, for example, would not serve its purpose if potential applicants cared about work-study opportunities and that category was not included.

A database model, or diagram, helps to avoid that problem by graphically displaying the categories and their relationships. In addition to providing a clear road map for the developers and pro-

GET STARTED NOW!

- In School: Math and other courses that emphasize logical thinking.
- After School: Offer to help a community organization organize its database.
- Around Town: Get "big picture" practice. Work with the organizing committee of an event that requires coordinating many people and activities such as fund-raisers, Special Olympics, or even prom.

grammers, the model also gives the client an opportunity to confirm that the development team understands his business and has included everything that might be needed.

The most common way for database modelers to create their diagrams is by using an entity-relationship model, or ERM. In plain language, that means that the diagram identifies things or categories of things that are important (the entities), the possible characteristics (attributes) for each entity, and the relationships among the entities.

For your hypothetical college database, some of the entities (categories) would be schools, majors, athletics, and location. Each entity would have attributes, or characteristics. The attributes of the school entity, for example, might include location, tuition, acceptance rate, average SAT score, and so on. For this database the relationships that define how the entities interact might include the requirement that each school must have one or more majors and that each major must have one or more schools. A school may not have more that one tuition level, but each tuition level may have many schools. It is easier to keep the terms straight when you remember that entities generally are nouns, and relationships usually include verbs.

Database modelers create their models by looking at the "big picture." They rely more on logic and abstract thinking to anticipate questions that the database might have to answer, rather than on the technical and detail-oriented skills that are critical for software developers and programmers. Some database modelers have come to the field with strong experience in business and problem solving, learning the technical aspects of the field after they were hired.

Data Visualization Specialist

It was so exciting to be elected to your town's council! But now your first meeting is turning into a real snooze fest. Bobby B, another representative, wants the group to support an increase in funding for senior citizen services. "In our town, 4 percent of residents are under the age of five, compared to 7 percent five years ago; 16 percent are between ages six and 18, compared to 17 percent five years ago…" and on and on and on. At this rate, who knows how long it will take to actually start talking about senior citizens! It's so boring that everyone seems to be struggling to stay awake.

Bobby worked hard on his speech, but it turned out to be more confusing than convincing. Most people just can't keep that many numbers in their heads, much less draw conclusions from them. However, most people can understand simple visual presentations. A pie chart showing seniors as a percent of the population this year and another showing the situation five years ago would have been much more effective for Bobby.

Too much information is a problem in many areas of our lives. The corporate world, with its powerful computers that collect, analyze, and report every detail of every business, is especially affected. Managers find themselves "drowning in data, but starv-

GET STARTED NOW!

- In School: Art and design, writing, business, and math.
- After School: Volunteer to make posters and other visual materials for a favorite club or candidate for student government.
- Around Town: Start a collection of data visualizations from newspapers and Web sites.

ing for knowledge." With all the information they receive, it is not easy to know what is important or how different statistics relate to each other.

Data visualization specialists translate complex data, concepts, and relationships into graphs, charts, and other visual representations. Visualizations make information easier to understand. They can also reveal relationships that may not have been noticed in text-only reports, help us truly understand the meaning of a commonly used word like "trillion," or see dozens of different ways to view a single topic like the 2010 Gulf oil spill.

Clear visual representations of information are profitable for businesses in other ways as well. By decreasing the time managers need to analyze data, companies move quickly to take advantage of current conditions. In addition, as business environments become increasingly multinational, multilingual, and multicultural, visual representations literally put all participants on the same page.

Data visualization specialists are aware that even the most standard formats for charts and graphs must be adapted for different situations. Plain, straightforward design may work for internal evaluation of a product's performance, but exciting colors and graphics can enhance the impact of a sales presentation, an advertisement, or a consumer education poster.

When there are huge amounts of information, even charts and graphs may not be able to make everything clear. Online displays of information allow users to select the information that is important to them. The 2009 Economic Stimulus Act, for example, included $787 billion in spending. Want to know where that money went? An interactive Web site includes every project and job that was funded, and users can inquire by category, state, congressional district, and even ZIP code. "A picture is worth a thousand words" (or numbers) is certainly true at http://www.recovery.gov.

Digital Forensics Expert

Five years ago you started Bright Ideas, an advertising agency. Bright Ideas was famous for extremely creative sales presentations, and almost every company that saw your work eventually hired you. This year Bright Ideas has been losing clients to a new agency, whose ideas were very similar to some that Bright Ideas was working on. You thought this strange and hired a digital forensics expert to investigate the situation. The expert was not too surprised when she found that the creative director of the new agency had once worked at Bright Ideas and was helping himself to ideas on your computers.

Like the teams on CSI shows, digital forensics experts find and retrieve evidence that can solve a crime, looking for clues in data stored on disks, CD-ROMs, and cell phones rather than in blood splatter and DNA. Like CSI teams, they are careful with evidence to ensure that their results will be admissible in court. They work with copies of hard drives and preserve the originals to refute any suggestion of tampering with evidence.

Data uncovered on a computer may include information about the people or activities in question, or evidence that the computer itself was for illegal activities, such as credit card fraud, theft of

CAREER 411

Search It!
Digital Forensics Association at http://www.digitalforensicsassociation.org.

Surf It!
Forensic Focus at http://www.forensicfocus.com.

Read It!
The Electronic Evidence Information Center at http://www.e-evidence.info/biblio.html.

Learn It!
Minimum Education: Bachelor's degree, plus certification in computer forensics.

Typical Majors: Computer science, information science, computer forensics.

Special Skills: Technical and analytical skills for a broad range of computer storage devices, operating systems, programming languages, and software applications; expertise in password cracking and file decryption software; and ability to serve (calmly and professionally) as an expert witness.

Earn It!
The median annual salary is $99,000.
(Source: http://www.indeed.com)

GET STARTED NOW!

- In School: Study computer hardware and software systems.
- After School: Check into the availability of local law enforcement explorer clubs at http://www.learningforlife.org.
- Around Town: Use the Internet to follow the digital trail of crimes and scandals you hear about in the news.

intellectual property, terrorism, or accessing another computer without official access.

Many of the clues found by forensics experts are in files that suspects think they have deleted. Instructing the computer to "delete" a file eliminates information that points the system to that file. The file itself still exists and can be located easily. Computers also retain a record of every site that has been accessed. That was useful in the case of Kathleen Savio, who drowned in her bathtub in March 2004. When high levels of sleeping pills were found in her body, her death was classified as a suicide. It was later reclassified as a homicide, however, when her husband's computer revealed his online search for painless killing methods.

A computer can serve as a tool to analyze information found on other computers. The Enron corporate fraud case, for example, included raw data equal to about 250 million pages of text if printed. Computers were able to find relationships and information that would have taken a very long time if done manually. In a similar way, computer analysis of paid claims has helped several insurance companies find many millions of dollars in fraudulent claims.

Other electronic devices, including cell phones, also retain information. E-mails, text messages, Web sites, videos, calendar information, and contacts have all been sources of important evidence in cases of corporate fraud, cyberbullying, drug dealing, and cheating spouses.

EVIDENCE   EVIDENCE   EVIDENCE   EVIDENCE

As a computer forensic expert, how could you use a game format to interest high school students in your career?

Your game should allow the students to experience the challenge of looking for clues on a computer, cell phone, or other electronic device. You may use a crime that was committed through the computer itself (hacking, theft of information, or credit card fraud) or a situation for which evidence was found on an electronic device (divorce, cyberbullying, or other criminal activity).

Create a gameboard with instructions that include a background story to set up the situation. For inspiration, check out these accounts of real computer forensic experiences at https://www.arsenalexperts.com/Case-Studies,http:// www.networkworld.com/slideshows/2008/121508-year-in-cybercrime.html#slide1; and http://burgessforensics.com/case_studies.php.

Computer forensic experts are patient and meticulous, often working alone as they sift through files. They are confident and well spoken, able to testify in court without being rattled by an aggressive defense attorney. And they know that when they want to eliminate information from a computer, the "delete" command is not the way to go.

Disaster Recovery Analyst

Have you seen any good disaster movies lately? You know…the ones in which Earth (or a substantial part of it) is destroyed (or nearly destroyed) by asteroids, earthquakes, aliens, mutant creatures, or any combination thereof?

In your profession a disaster is anything that interferes with an organization's ability to function as it usually does. While a building fire, local earthquake, or computer virus may not be as dramatic as depicted in the movies, any one of them can have a huge impact on a company, its customers and employees, and possibly the entire country.

Each new client is a learning experience. You assess the potential risks, including those related to climate and geology, industry legal requirements, and the way the company uses technology. You learn everything about how each process or department works, and what a loss of functioning in each one would mean to the overall organization. Most companies, for example, can tolerate downtime in advertising or accounting more easily than a breakdown in customer service communications technology. All of this research is essential for your business impact analysis, a document that helps management set priorities for recovery.

GET STARTED NOW!

- In School: Computer science, writing, communications.
- After School: Participate in any activity that allows you to use your skills in getting people to cooperate on a project.
- Around Town: Check the Web sites of public services (local and state government, police, fire, school district, and others), utilities (such as gas and water), and other facilities to see if they have disaster recovery plans.

Using your impact analysis, you develop a disaster recovery plan, which includes ongoing preparation and practice in addition to specific policies, instructions, routines, and guidelines for recovery from disaster.

IF YOU WERE. . .

As a disaster recovery analyst, how could you determine the level of disaster planning for the information technology systems of local businesses?

. . . MAKE IT REAL!

Put together a short survey (five to ten questions) about disaster recovery plans with multiple-choice answers. The survey should include the things that you believe to be most critical in a disaster recovery plan. HINT: You can get ideas from the Web sites that are suggested here and from the recommendations offered by the Federal Emergency Management Agency (FEMA) at http://www.ready. gov/business and http://www.fema.gov/business.

Create a list of businesses and agencies that you would like to include in your study. Include a wide variety, such as government, religious institutions, school districts, doctors, dentists, hospitals, community centers, local television and radio stations, etc.

Write a cover letter explaining that you are a high school student and would appreciate their participation in your career exploration project. Be sure that the surveys include contact information (mailing address, fax, e-mail) that responders can use to get it back to you.

Tally the results! If your research shows that your community is extremely well prepared (or extremely unprepared), you might want to write an article about what you discovered for a local newspaper or a disaster planning Web site.

Two critical components of the plan are establishing procedures for storing critical information offsite and for meeting immediate business needs. Businesses such as banks and hospitals, which cannot have any downtime, usually establish hot sites, facilities that are always available and able to take over immediately. They may also use mirroring software, ensuring that the backup is constantly synchronized with the primary site. Businesses that can tolerate downtime often use warm sites, locations that have desks, phones, and desktop computers, but not access to all of the company's technology. Businesses with little dependence on technology may use cold sites, empty rooms to which equipment can be delivered when needed.

Because most companies place the safety of employees and their families above every other priority, you work with senior management to develop policies such as criteria for closing or evacuating the facilities, procedures for communicating with employees after a disaster, and a line of succession for making executive decisions if the head of the company is unavailable.

All of your recommendations eventually go into a book that becomes the company's "bible" for disaster preparedness and recovery. This bible must be kept up-to-date and updated immediately if there are changes in staff or systems. Every employee should understand the book's contents and know where to locate a copy. Finally, the company must commit to scheduled practices to ensure that every employee is competent and confident in his or her recovery role, and to identify omissions, errors, or unclear instructions before those instructions are actually needed.

"Hope for the best, but prepare for the worst" is one of those old sayings that is more appropriate today than ever.

E-Commerce Entrepreneur

As is often the case with successful entrepreneurs, it all started with a random idea. Your friend Sofia needed to find a gift for her grandparents' anniversary. Surfing the Net, she found a die-cast model of a 1968 Ford Mustang GT, an exact replica of their first car. How perfect! In the course of her search Sofia came across several sites aimed at "baby boomers," people in her grandparents' age group. She would have shared them with her grandparents, but they were all pretty dull and boring.

Wow! This could be her chance to start her own business. She was definitely qualified for it. She had experience in marketing, loved shopping online, was independent, organized, and energetic, and now had a great idea.

Her initial research showed that "boomers" were very active online purchasers. She would target that group, offering models of cars from the 1950s and 1960s, music, comedy, candy, and other memorabilia of the "good old days."

Sofia also discovered that Web sites offering content are generally more successful than those offering only products. She decided her site would include content. The sections she designed for humorous memories of the old days, crabby comments about today's prices, trivia, and bargain tips got rave reviews from her grandparents and their friends.

GET STARTED NOW!

- In School: Writing, accounting, business math, design.
- After School: Volunteer to help keep your school's Web site up-to-date.
- Around Town: Compare a local business with both an onsite and online presence.

CAREER 411

Search It!
Check out the eCommerce Merchants Trade Association at http://www.ecmta.org.

Surf It!
See what you can learn about business failures at http://www.businesspundit.com/25-internet-startups-that-bombed-miserably, and learn about successes at http://onlinebusiness.about.com/od/successstories/Online_Business_Success_Stories.htm.

Read It!
Practical eCommerce at http://www.practicalecommerce.com.

Learn It!
Minimum Education: No formal education requirements.

Typical Majors: It's helpful to have an understanding of marketing, design, writing, HTML, and the basics of business management.

Special Skills: Business savvy, risk taker, innovator, and hard worker.

Earn It!
Salaries for this profession vary wildly by business.

Once she completed a business plan that described her vision and her estimates of costs and revenue, Sofia knew it was time to find someone who knew about setting up a Web site and how the Internet actually worked. Sofia put in a call to you, her pal the Web site developer.

You agreed to help, warning Sofia she would be getting assignments from you. Her first task was to go to an online company that maintains a database of every domain name (URL for a site), find a name that no one else had, and register it immediately. You helped her with the other administrative tasks: selecting a hosting service (to provide space on a server and give her access to the Web), creating a merchant account (to accept credit card payments), choosing a shopping cart program (to collect the order information), selecting software to process the sale and send the

information to her bank and the customer's, and getting an SSL (secure sockets layer, which is a secure server that encrypts data to ensure security).

The next decisions were up to Sofia: whether or not to charge for shipping, where to keep her inventory, and how to get it to customers. She developed a marketing plan with strategies to make her site known to potential customers and then to get those customers to keep coming back. She hired a search engine optimization specialist to help her get a good spot in a Google search. With your technical knowledge and her creativity, the two of you designed an impressive Web site, making sure to include the required privacy and usage policies and the copyright information.

Working on this project with Sofia was a lot of fun. Her site has been running for almost a year now. Sofia is happy, spending her days (and nights) finding and photographing new products, fulfilling orders, taking phone calls, keeping the financial records, and writing for the content sections. Your only question is whether Sofia will have time to hang out with you again before you both qualify as "old timers."

Hardware Engineer

Every computer, from the largest to the tiniest, is made up of two components: software that runs the programs on the computer, and hardware that includes the physical elements of the computer itself. Hardware, in turn, includes the core elements of the computer (the computer chips, circuit boards, and memory and storage units) and the peripherals or the devices that are connected to the computer (the keyboards, mice, modems, and printers).

Hardware engineers help companies design new computers to solve new types of problems. They also modify or redesign existing equipment to improve efficiency, size, performance, or safety. To accomplish these goals, hardware engineers use mathematical models, simulations, and their knowledge of software, electronics, and physics. They also use "reverse engineering," which means finding something that is close to what they want to accomplish, taking it apart to understand the underlying technology, and then creating something new based on the same principles.

Suppose you were a hardware engineer, assigned to build a system that will meet defined objectives. After many calculations, you are pretty sure you have developed a solution. Your next step would be to create a prototype, or sample, for the end users to review,

GET STARTED NOW!

- In School: Computer science, math (algebra, geometry, trigonometry, and calculus), and science (biology, chemistry, and physics).
- After School: Visit local computer repair shops. If they will let you have some of the discarded computers that they have replaced, try to take them apart and reconstruct them.
- Around Town: How many things can you find in your home that use microprocessors?

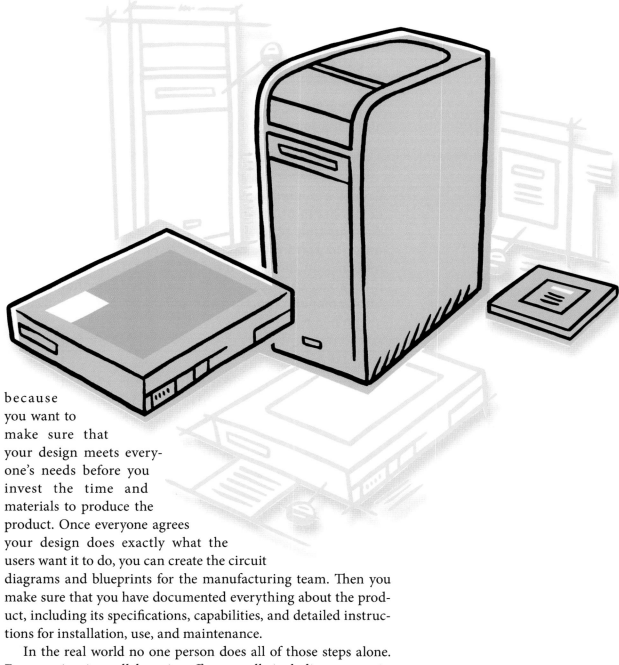

because
you want to
make sure that
your design meets every-
one's needs before you
invest the time and
materials to produce the
product. Once everyone agrees
your design does exactly what the
users want it to do, you can create the circuit
diagrams and blueprints for the manufacturing team. Then you
make sure that you have documented everything about the product, including its specifications, capabilities, and detailed instructions for installation, use, and maintenance.

In the real world no one person does all of those steps alone.
Every project is a collaborative effort, usually including experts in
software design, marketing, security, and manufacturing. You are
a success in this field because you are skilled in problem solving,
electrical engineering, programming, and computer-aided design.

You realize, though, that those technical skills would not be very important if you did not also have excellent interpersonal skills. It is because you are known as someone who can work well as part of a team and who can communicate clearly and easily with nontechnical people that you are in demand by many types of end users, as well as by the teams that manage security and disaster recovery plans.

Hardware engineers have also contributed by making computer components smaller and smaller, resulting in flat screen TVs and monitors, tiny flash drives, cell phones, and digital cameras.

Computers have evolved from room-size machines with more than 18,000 vacuum tubes to tiny microchips that can be embedded in products. In 1970, the smallest microchip was the size of a postage stamp and contained 1,000 transistors. By 2010 a chip that size could hold 32 billion transistors.

Today microprocessors are in everything from microwaves to medical equipment. As long as engineers can keep increasing the number of transistors on a chip, technology will keep increasing, costs will decrease, and performance will increase. It is hard to imagine where hardware technology will take us next.

Health Informatics Specialist

If you have ever been to a doctor, there is probably a paper folder in her office full of information about your medical history. The information may be on computer printouts, or on notes written in your doctor's scrawl using abbreviations known only to her. The emergency room you visited after your vacation mishap had no information about you, so they created a folder for you at that facility. (At least you remembered to give them your allergy information!) As did the specialist you saw at home and the hospital where you had surgery.

Imagine all those folders just for you, each filed wherever it was created. Then try to imagine the number of folders for older people. By the time a person reaches mature years there is information in so many places, with no way for health care providers to access, organize, or share that information with a patient's other providers.

Someone needed to organize things. The obvious choice was information technology and computer science professionals, people who were trained and experienced in managing information. They in turn strongly recommended establishing an electronic database. Technology professionals who were "bilingual" in tech-

GET STARTED NOW!

- In School: Take computer classes, biology, and math.
- After School: Volunteer at your local hospital.
- Around Town: Next time you visit your physician or dentist, ask if they are using or plan to start using electronic health records.

CAREER 411

Search It!
American Health Information Management Association at http://www.ahima.org.

Surf It!
Learn more about health informatics careers at http://hicareers.com.

Read It!
The Office of the National Coordinator for Health Information Technology at http://healthit.hhs.gov.

Learn It!
Minimum Education: Bachelor's or master's degree.

Typical Majors: Information technology, health informatics.

Special Skills: Attention to detail, organized, able to process and track large amounts of information, creative thinking (especially related to computer problems), excellent verbal and written communication skills, with ability to explain complicated material to any end user.

Earn It!
The median annual salary is $84,270.
(Source: U.S. Department of Labor)

nology and in insurance/medicine were critical in helping the two groups communicate their needs and abilities to each other.

Because professionals qualified in both areas were not very common, the science of health informatics emerged to train people in a new field that combines technology, health care, and business management.

A key piece of the effort is converting the folder system to electronic health records (EHR). Imagine if every contact with a health care provider were immediately recorded in an electronic database, we would be able to access our entire heath history at any time and from any place. In addition to providing convenience, a central system could improve patient safety. A doctor or pharmacist, for example, could be notified immediately if he tried to write or fill a prescription that was not safe to combine with other medications or conditions. This conversion to electronic records is so important that Congress included $19 billion in the 2009 economic stimulus bill to help doctors and hospitals design, implement, and secure EHR systems.

Health informatics specialists are critical to the planning, development, and implementation of new software. Because of their familiarity with the medical world, they can work with physicians, nurses, and hospital personnel to identify their needs. Because of their technical expertise, they can develop a plan in terms that programmers can work with easily.

Health informatics requires a genuine interest in health care. Many people in the field are physicians, nurses, pharmacists, or hospital administrators who are also very attracted to technology. People whose initial strengths are technological must have a very strong interest in health care. And those who plan a health informatics career in the future now have a wide range of undergraduate and master's programs specifically designed for this specialty.

Surf It!
Test your cyber-crime IQ at http://investigation.discovery.com/investigation/quiz-central/famous-crimes/id-theft.html and http://news.discovery.com/tech/cyber-crime-quiz.html.

Read It!
IT Security at http://www.itsecurity.com.

Learn It!
Minimum Education: Bachelor's or master's degree.

Typical Majors: Computer science, human-computer interaction (HCI), information design.

Special Skills: Curious and perceptive, excellent ability to relate to people, good written communication skills, familiarity with the product or service being evaluated. Certified Information System Security Professional (CISSP) certification and participation in professional associations recommended.

Earn It!
The median annual salary is $75,660.
(Source: U.S. Department of Labor)

Information Security Specialist

You probably interact with the Internet dozens of times each day, using it as a source of entertainment, communication, information, or purchasing. Each of your interactions creates data that is stored on a computer. Unfortunately there are people who try to access that data to spy on a business competitor, steal from an employer or supplier, or capture customer information to access credit cards or investment accounts.

Information security specialists protect and preserve information about an organization, its customers, and its vendors. They anticipate every possible way someone could gain access to information. Their work ranges from securing the networks transmitting data, to implementing policies for lost or stolen laptops and regulating employees' use of company computers.

Information security specialists focus on the principles known as the CIA triad: confidentiality (preventing unauthorized disclosure or destruction of information), integrity (protecting the accuracy and completeness of data and the methods used to process it), and availability (ensuring that systems and information are available and usable when needed).

Their projects typically begin with an evaluation of the current systems, identifying the most likely types of threats, the sources of threats, and the weak links where a threat could enter. And

GET STARTED NOW!

- In School: Computer classes, writing, and speech.
- After School: Join your school's computer club.
- Around Town: Search the Internet for news of widespread cyber attacks.

because even the best plans can have failures, they also detail the requirements for backup systems and data recovery plans.

Threats to computer systems fall into three categories: cyber attacks, cyber theft, and other threats. Cyber attacks are crimes that target the computer system itself, use viruses, Trojan horses, and electronic vandalism or sabotage. Cyber thefts use the computer as a tool to steal money, intellectual property, or financial data. "Other threats" include spyware, adware, hacking, phishing, or spoofing.

Strangers or competitors are obvious sources of threats. Security specialists usually address those threats with technical controls such as firewalls, encryption, and special coding. Recently terminated employees are another source of threats. Unless their access codes are immediately closed, they can easily steal information or damage information networks. Such actions have been estimated to cost the business community as much as one trillion dollars.

Current employees may be an unintentional source of threats, introducing bugs or creating access to the company's computers by using company computers to check their personal e-mail or surf the Internet, or by using (or losing) a memory stick at home. Security specialists protect against accidental employee security breaches by physically limiting access to some computers, by installing anti-virus software, and by requiring frequent password changes. They may also tighten administrative policies, initiate audits, and increase employee training in computer systems security.

Employees may also compromise information as unknowing victims of social engineering, a scam that tricks people into breaking the normal security rules. Social engineering can take many forms. Impersonation is one such form which involves someone pretending to be someone a person is likely to trust or obey to get access to sensitive information. Due to the human tendency to believe people are who they say they are this method has been used to connect with hundreds of people from military, intelligence, and information security sources, some of whom divulged personal or sensitive information without taking precautions to identify whether or not the requests for information were coming from a legitimate source. Information security specialists know that even personnel who should know better can benefit from frequent training and reminders.

Information Technology Auditor

After so many years working as an information technology (IT) auditor, you are no longer surprised when employees at your client's companies are not delighted to see you. Those reactions are not personal; they just reflect the fact that most people don't like to have their work or procedures examined. Auditing can include in-depth examination of the organization's databases, networks, hardware, software, encryption, compliance with legal regulations, and disaster recovery plans.

Auditors are hired to identify risks to the business' information, and therefore to the business itself. They ensure that the information systems meet the three requirements needed for total confidence. These critical elements, sometimes referred to as the CIA triad, include: confidentiality (the information in the systems will be disclosed only to authorized users), integrity (the information provided by the system will be accurate and reliable), and availability (the computer systems will be available whenever they are required).

GET STARTED NOW!

- In School: Math, statistics, computer technology, accounting.
- After School: Clubs that give you the experience of running a business, such as Junior Achievement (http://www.ja.org) or DECA (http://www.deca.org), if offered in your area.
- Around Town: Take note of consistent types of service you receive when you visit chain stores and fast food restaurants.

CAREER 411

Search It!
ISACA at http://www.isaca.org/.

Surf It!
Learn more about typical IT security audit findings at http://www.maxi-pedia.com/IT+security+audit+findings.

Read It!
See the basics of an information systems audit at http://www.csoonline.com/article/492804/information-systems-audit-the-basics and an IT security audit checklist at http://www.brighthub.com/computing/enterprise-security/articles/70931.aspx.

Learn It!
Minimum Education: Bachelor's degree plus certification.

Typical Majors: Information systems management.

Special Skills: Independent, organized, strong written and verbal communication skills, excellent problem-solving abilities, ability to work alone or on a team.

Earn It!
The median annual salary is $70,000.

(Source: http://www.simplyhired.com)

In the initial phase of an audit, you and your client agree on a scope statement that outlines the objectives of the project and budgeted time or money. From that you create an audit plan, describing how you will meet the objectives. Your plan includes the specific processes or business segments that will be audited and identifies the people, processes, and equipment that are involved with those objectives.

Clients usually designate someone from their IT area to be your contact, providing background information, explaining policies and processes, and facilitating your communication with other members of the department. As you interview each person identified in your audit plan, you look for anything that might indicate a gap in security or control. You also collect and evaluate tangible evidence from the system itself, checking that calculations are correct, the process is effective and efficient, and there are no patterns or trends that might indicate fraud. For some purposes you may use standard software; for others you may write a program that creates dummy information that allows you to evaluate a specific segment of the system.

To complete your assignment you create and submit an audit report that includes the conclusions you have reached based on your interviews, investigations, and assessments. If you have concerns about one (or more) of the areas you audited, you include a factual description of the evidence you found and your professional opinion about the risks connected with that situation. As an auditor, you may recommend solutions, but it is management's job to implement them. If you find evidence of fraud, your job is only to document that evidence; the company is responsible for further investigation.

In addition to current assignments, you must stay on top of the constant changes in information technology. If you specialize in a specific industry (such as banking or manufacturing), you also keep up with changes in that industry. Your love of learning new things and solving problems are among the reasons you are still excited about your career.

Information Technology Consultant

Congratulations! Now that you have a few years of information technology (IT) work under your belt, you are ready to go out on your own as an independent IT consultant. Independent consultants help clients install, maintain, adapt, or secure their IT hardware and software. They also serve as management consultants, advising clients on business issues and proposing suitable IT solutions.

Consulting has a lot to offer. You set your own hours and there are always new challenges to keep things exciting. Plus, your success or failure results from your actions, not the company's revenue or the newest management team's vision. Another challenge, however, is that consultants cannot count on getting the same paycheck every two weeks, or getting paid for sick days or vacation time.

It's a tough (and risky) decision to break out on one's own and become an independent IT consultant. But the work you do as a consultant is similar to that of an employee. You solve problems the same way, by researching the situation and doing some orga-

GET STARTED NOW!

- In School: Computer classes, writing, and any classes that require oral reports.
- After School: See how it feels to come in as an "expert." Volunteer to tutor younger kids in their school or at a community organization.
- Around Town: Seek out opportunities to share your computer expertise with people you know that are older or younger than you.

nized, logical analysis. Your research includes a little online digging and some networking to find IT consultants to interview.

Almost everything you find online urges new consultants to specialize, either in a field of technical expertise (such as information or network security, social media management, quality assurance, or business intelligence) or in an industry (health care, banking, video games, or retail). Some consultants even specialize in a skill within an industry such as enterprise software or cloud computing.. Consultants who specialize are better able to stay current in their field and to establish the credibility that potential clients seek.

The real key to success as an information technology consultant lies in marketing yourself. Besides having a logo, business cards, and stationery, you need to keep your name in the public eye. That means writing articles for trade journals and Web sites, creating a Web site or blog for yourself, joining trade associations, and doing lots and lots of networking.

In the consulting world, personal skills are more important than they have been in any place you have ever worked. Every client wants to feel cared for and well taken care of.

Clients usually pay by the hour, so they want you to be organized, goal directed, and energetic whenever you are onsite. Information technology consultants who are especially likeable often find that their clients hire them for future projects and recommend them to colleagues.

To be successful and happy in this type of work, you must be comfortable with two things: stress and financial uncertainty. You have to accept that there will be emergencies from some clients when you are working with others, and that you will never be able to schedule clients for 52 weeks a year. And you should be able to thrive in an environment of deadlines and constant change.

Should you become a consultant or remain an employee? The industry needs both, so either way the career opportunities are there for you. It's up to you to decide whether working on staff or being an independent consultant best fits your personality and skills. Be honest with yourself, and take time to consider which direction will ultimately be the best fit for you.

Information Technology Project Manager

For the past year, everyone at Lovely Cosmetics has been frustrated with the company's information systems. Financial information, inventory management, and marketing are managed independently. Information from one system is not always consistent with another, and data from different systems cannot be combined for more useful analysis. Unless these issues can be resolved, the company's profitability will be endangered. Project Lovelier has been approved as an effort to create one integrated system.

You, a systems analyst, will be the project manager. Your responsibilities include keeping the project on track, coordinating the various segments, and ensuring that all of the objectives are met.

Like all projects, Project Lovlier includes specific objectives, a well-defined beginning and end, and a dedicated team. As project manager, you have to control the four critical factors: people, cost, time, and scope. The riskiest factor is the last one. "Scope creep" occurs when so many users request so many little changes and additions (without additional time or money) that the project eventually becomes unmanageable.

GET STARTED NOW!

- In School: Computer, business, and writing classes.
- After School: Practice organization and planning in everything you do, from cleaning your room to preparing a meal.
- Around Town: Help coordinate fund-raisers and holiday parties to get some practice as a project manager.

CAREER 411

Search It!
Project Management Institute at http://www.pmi.org.

Surf It!
Check out *Baseline* magazine's project section at http://www.baselinemag.com.

Read It!
Peruse project case studies at http://www.pmi.org/en/Business-Solutions/OPM3-Case-Study-Library.aspx.

Learn It!
Minimum Education: Bachelor's degree or master's in business administration (MBA).

Typical Majors: Computer science, information technology, business administration.

Special Skills: Expertise with networks and databases, and estimating and budgeting, and solid background in information technology. Organized, strong analytical skills, and able to motivate and manage people.

Earn It!
The median annual salary is $82,443.
(Source: http://www.payscale.com)

You divide your assignment into five distinct phases. The first, defining the project, can take the longest. The team meets with everyone who will be affected by the final product. Wisely, you have included nontechnical people on the team. They contribute to the team's productivity by clarifying user needs.

The second phase of the project is planning. The technical people develop a step-by-step plan, breaking each step into even smaller pieces. For each substep there is a description, an allocation of work hours (including allowances for the unexpected), and an identification of the other steps it is dependent upon or influences. The team also agrees on quality checkpoints. By now there are so many details that you begin to use a project management program to ensure that you can monitor all of the activities that overlap or follow each other.

An additional aspect of planning is meeting with management, end users, and developers until everyone agrees on exactly what Project Lovelier will include. This formal approval is your best insurance against scope creep, giving you a way to diplomatically turn down the "I forgot to mention..." requests that almost always turn up.

During the third phase, execution of the plan, the actual work takes place. You have to stay on your toes to manage the people, cost, and time. Some things have to be moved around and tweaked, but eventually it all comes together. Monitoring and controlling, the fourth phase, is closely connected to execution. Some sections may be ready for testing while others are still in the earlier stages, but eventually everything is installed, tested, and ready to roll.

The team is ready for the celebration, but not before closure, the fifth phase. Your project management software creates reports of everything that was done and how each objective was met. Post-mortem scope creep is still possible until everyone signs off on the closure document.

Now it's time for that celebration!

Intrusion Detection Analyst

It might seem that intrusions (unauthorized access into a computer or network) would be obvious most of the time. If a computer gets a virus, the fact that the computer does something very strange, or stops working entirely, should be enough of a clue. If only it were that simple! A virus needs a trigger to set it off. That trigger may depend on something in the future, a specific date, or an action by the user. Or, the intrusion may never affect the computer at all; it may *only* steal trade secrets or customers' confidential information. As an intrusion detection analyst, your job has three major components: preventing intrusions, detecting them quickly (so that an information thief does not have time to do damage and cause a virus to spread), and resolving the issues caused by intrusions.

Individuals concerned about unauthorized entry into their homes install burglar alarms to alert them if such entry does occur. You install intrusion detection software, the computer version of a burglar alarm. The most common way for software to detect an intrusion is by using a signature-based model that inspects files, seeking patterns like those used in known malware (an abbreviation for malicious software). Another detection option uses an anomaly threat model that analyzes all network traffic to identify anything that differs from the usual size or flow.

GET STARTED NOW!

- In School: Math, writing, computer classes.
- After School: Join any activity that requires you to practice speaking in front of others. Consider clubs, such as debate, drama, etc.
- Around Town: Pay attention to what businesses and homeowners do to protect their property and think about how these strategies translate into technology.

Although a burglar alarm tells us that someone has entered our home, we would prefer to prevent that entry from occurring in the first place. We address prevention by strengthening our security measures. Similarly, you protect your computers with intrusion prevention software and penetration testing analyses (tests that identify weak spots in the system that can be used for access). You may also use honeypots, which are programs that serve as bait for attackers. Because honeypots have no other function, attempts to access them imply that someone is exploring your system. Although they can collect useful information about intruders, honeypots can also increase security risk in other ways, so you use them very carefully.

If an intruder does get into the house or computer, someone has to respond to it. Your first priority is preventing the problem from getting worse. Then you repair the damage, using computer forensics techniques to determine how the attack was able to happen. Finally you create an incident report, describing what happened, what you learned, and what steps can prevent it from happening again.

In smaller organizations the responsibilities of your job might be part of another job, such as information security or computer forensics. Your job may also have a different title, such as threat detection or forensics information security analyst.

Network Administrator

It's been one of those days, the kind when just about anything that can go wrong, does go wrong. At 3:00 P.M. you're finally at your desk, ready to get into the lunch you've been thinking about for the past two hours, when a tech from your group calls with news that the company's network has crashed. You shift into your "code blue" mode, like a doctor or nurse learning of a critical care situation. As always you are calm and confident, at least on the outside, a technique that you know will help everyone focus on the job. The good news is that the backup system you have already set up is in place, so little or no data will be lost.

Your team knows the routine: meet to brainstorm about possible causes of the failure and then divide up the tasks to check each possibility. The phone calls have already begun; everyone in the organization wants to know when they can get back to work. Knowing the way that false assurances can backfire, you promise to get back to each caller as soon as you know anything.

As expected, someone on your team eventually finds the problem. You make the correction, test it several times, and the company is, literally, back in business.

System crashes are definitely a jolt of adrenaline, but you stay busy even when everything is performing perfectly. Your primary responsibility is to ensure the safety, functionality, and availability of all of the organization's networks.

GET STARTED NOW!

- In School: Take as many computer classes as possible.
- After School: Offer to help people set up or troubleshoot their home computer networks.
- Around Town: Browse the aisles of a local computer store to keep up with the latest technologies.

CAREER 411

Search It!
Network Professional Association at http://www.npanet.org and Network World at http://www.networkworld.com.

Surf It!
Find out what happens to e-mail after it is sent at http://www.thenetworkadministrator.com/secretlifeofemail.htm.

Read It!
Find tutorials about computer networks at http://www.buzzle.com/articles/computer-networking-basics.html and http://www.buzzle.com/articles/router-vs-switch-vs-hub.html.

Learn It!
Minimum Education: Bachelor's degree plus certification.

Typical Majors: Computer science, information science, and management information systems.

Special Skills: Strong analytical and problem-solving skills, communication skills, ability to work as part of a team, and understanding of the business that the network supports.

Earn It!
The median annual salary is $69,160.
(Source: U.S. Department of Labor)

A computer network is a system that connects computers so they can share information and resources. Applications and data are stored on the network's server, rather than on individual computers, and are accessible by any authorized user. When the network does not function properly, everything stops and the cost to the organization can be staggering.

To keep everything running, you constantly monitor all hardware and software, performing maintenance tasks, and reconfiguring the network when necessary. You develop, install, and maintain emergency and backup routines. You also administer the organization's e-mail system, create and delete individual user accounts, and improve security through firewalls, and by enabling individual users to access only authorized specific files and programs.

The network includes hardware (interface cards, repeaters, hubs, switches, bridges, and routers and software), and software that installs components or adjusts settings. For example, the operating system of a router or switch controls access to the network or firewall settings. Another type of systems software is diagnostic applications, programs used to provide the data that evaluates the system's performance, identifies future needs, and determines network requirements.

As a network administrator, you can never say that you know everything about the career. Because of the constant change, you have to make an effort to stay current with the standards, technology, and practices in specialized areas ranging from network configuration to e-mail security.

Robotics Software Engineer

In 1969 the most advanced computers in the world helped bring humans to the moon for the first time. Back then computers were very expensive, and were only in large businesses and research facilities where trained experts could use them. Today computers are everywhere. They are affordable, easy to use, and much more powerful than they were in those days. In fact, your digital camera or cell phone has about a million times more RAM than the computer on the Apollo spaceship.

Many people believe that the robots will develop in the same way. Although robots are currently used primarily in military, manufacturing, and hospital environments, we are already beginning to see them in home applications. And research is even developing robots that can show emotions.

Creating a robot is definitely a team experience. Programmers usually specialize in design (the basic plans), control systems (how the robot will move), or user interface (how users will give instructions to the robot or get information from it). Other programmers test for errors in the software or simulate how the robot will behave.

GET STARTED NOW!

- In School: Math, calculus, trigonometry, physics, and any available computer programming classes.
- After School: Join any robotics competition teams in your area. If there are none, look for a teacher who might want to sponsor a team from FIRST (http://www.usfirst.org) or BEST Robotics (http://best.eng.auburn.edu).
- Around Town: Look at local businesses and create a list of tasks for which robots might helpful.

As with all software projects, the first step in developing a new robot is the planning. Marketing and project management specialists usually meet with clients to determine exactly what is needed.

If you were a robotics software engineer, you would work with mechanical and electrical engineers to create a detailed design to meet the client's needs. Although your primary expertise is in programming, it is very important that you have an understanding of those other specialties so that you can understand what the engineers are saying and explain what you are doing in terms that they can understand. You also need to know everything about the client's environment. For example, a project that involves controlling robots moving around a warehouse to get products that will be shipped to customers has to include ways to ensure that each robot selects the most efficient route, that the robots do not run into each other (or anything else in the warehouse), and that there is a way to give remote commands to the robots.

Once all the planning is completed and documented in detail, you would begin to write the actual software. Because programming robots can be so complex, you often use "pseudo code," a technique that is a combination of programming language and human language. Using pseudo code means that you can more easily look for problems in your commands and processes before you translate everything into programming language.

Looking for problems means testing and adjusting, and then testing and adjusting again until you are certain that the program does what it is supposed to do. Only when you are totally satisfied with the software can the actual production of the robot begin.

You agree with the robotics software engineers who say that the best part of their job is seeing the machine they worked on actually perform. Although there has been nothing quite like seeing your first robot in action, the thrill of watching every project "come to life" never gets old.

Robotics Technologist

Have you ever noticed that things almost always break at the worst possible time? Your computer freezes just when you are about to print out the paper that is due in an hour. Your car's tire goes flat just as you are ready to leave for a long weekend.

There's never a good time for a robot to break down. A robot that should be performing surgery, building a car, or working with an autistic child causes a lot of disruption when it suddenly can't do its job. And repairing a robot isn't something that just anyone can do. Keeping robots up and running is what robotics technicians do.

Odyssey Baking, for example, depends on its robots for a range of tasks, from assembling the crème-filled sandwich cookies to every stage of packaging and shipping. Because their robots are so critical, Odyssey employs technologists who are always onsite and available.

As one of those technologists, you devote much of your time to maintenance, ensuring that the robots function smoothly and last for a long time. When an Odyssey robot does malfunction, you quickly switch from maintenance mode to diagnose-and-repair mode.

Your ability to diagnose and repair problems is a result of your education and experience with electronics, hydraulics, and pneumatics, and your expertise with specialized equipment such as multimeters, oscilloscopes, flow meters, and hydraulic testing tools, as well as basic hand tools.

You also have a thorough understanding of each of the robot's components. These critical elements, common to most robots, often mimic human components that perform similar functions. Like humans, robots have a structure, or body, that gives them their form. They may have arms and joints to perform tasks, just as humans have elbows, wrists, and fingers. Sensors, similar to human senses, provide important information about the environment, including speed, orientation, the presence of other objects, and sometimes even light, chemical, sonar, or other cues. Actuators, the robot version of human muscles, make joints move and wheels spin. All of these components get their instructions from the controller, a programmed computer or microprocessor. Finally a robot needs power, usually provided by electricity, but sometimes by air, water pressure, or solar energy.

You also work with mechanical and electronics engineers when Odyssey Baking orders a new robot, ensuring that the robot meets the company's needs. While the manufacturer may have put together some of the new robot's systems, you supervise the team that completes the assembly (there

may be up to 2,000 individual parts) and installs the robot. At
the end of 2008 there were already 8.6 million robots in use, and
industry keeps finding even more uses for them. You've chosen a
good field; the need for robot technologists will not disappear any
time soon.

Search Engine Optimization Specialist

Aren't search engines amazing? They make it possible for almost anyone to find information about almost anything in just seconds. Google was not the first search engine, and it is not the only one. But it is the biggest. Back in 1998 Google could process 10,000 searches a day. That was impressive at the time, but nothing like the 34,000 searches it could do each second in 2010. Google, like most search engines, returns so many results for most questions that users often experience "search engine fatigue" after the first two pages.

Companies look to search engine optimization (SEO) specialists like you to improve the chances that their sites will appear in the beginning of search results so they can attract customers. You are usually pretty successful in doing that, thanks to your skills in mathematical analysis and creative puzzle solving.

The key to your job is to understand how search engines work. For example, when Google does a search, it does not actually look at every possible page. Instead it uses software "spiders" that crawl through the billions of Web pages, sending information to software that creates an index which lists every page. For an actual search, query software goes to the index, a faster solution than

GET STARTED NOW!

- In School: Writing, statistics, and design classes.
- After School: Practice nonfiction writing—write letters to the editor of your local newspaper, letters to magazines, posts to blogs or Web sites.
- Around Town: Search for various types of local business and see how high they are ranked in Google rankings.

going to the original pages. Relevant pages are selected and displayed. The order in which they are listed is determined by the score that Google's formulas assign.

Google does not reveal the complete details of its ranking formulas. As a professional SEO, however, you know some of the criteria that are used and you make sure your clients' pages take advantage of that information. One way a page can get extra points from Google is by having links to it from many other pages. But the number of links helps only if those other sites are of high quality themselves. The formula is similar to the way people act. You may go to a movie that a respected friend suggests, but avoid one that an unsavory person sitting outside the theater recommends.

There is a lot of variety in your job. You serve your existing clients by creating links and backlinks for their pages. You meet with potential clients, analyze reports to see if different key words might give better results, and adjust the design of pages where some elements might be hurting their ranking. You also create content for the sites of some clients, another way to improve ranking, as long as the content is useful, interesting, and includes the right key words. While doing all of that, you constantly check on the results your actions have had for your clients, as well as movements in the rankings of their competitors.

Committing time to your own blog and Web site is also important. You need to have high rankings to attract new business, so you do the same kind of work for yourself as you would for your paying clients.

Simulation Designer

In Nebraska, where you grew up, sailing was not a major activity, or even a minor one. So when you were assigned to be the lead designer on a simulation for Smooth Sailing, a school for beginning and advanced sailors, you knew you would have a lot to learn. In learning new skills, "practice makes perfect" is usually a good approach. It is not possible, though, when the actual experience is too expensive, too dangerous, or too complex for practice.

Simulations, interactive representations of the real world, allow practice when the real world does not. Simulations create safe environments, in which bad decisions do not cause planes to crash or patients to die. Users can experiment, seeing the results of different actions, or manipulate weather or other conditions.

Military training often uses simulations. Personnel who train with urban warfare simulation, which includes the almost-real sights, sounds, and unpredictability of battle, often develop a level of confidence in their own skills and their understanding of battle strategies and team coordination, to the point that in actual battle their responses are especially calm and effective. Crane operators who train with simulation are able to try different actions and experience consequences that they might prefer to avoid in real life. Through that trial-and-error experience, they often become highly flexible in finding solutions to unanticipated problems.

GET STARTED NOW!

- In School: Physics, math, computer science.
- After School: Get involved in helping to design your school newspaper or yearbook.
- Around Town: Start developing a good eye for design by noticing what designers do to create eye-catching signs, billboards, Web sites, and publications.

CAREER 411

Search It!
National Center for Simulation at http://www.simulationinformation.com.

Surf It!
Check out two simulations: Lemonade Stand at http://www.lemonadegame.com and Designing and Testing a Catapult at http://www.forgefx.com/casestudies/prenticehall/ph/catapult/design-test-simulation.htm.

Read It!
Find demos of simulations and descriptions of industries using simulations at http://www.forgefx.com/demos.htm.

Learn It!
Minimum Education: Bachelor's or master's degree.

Typical Majors: Operations research and systems, computer science, industrial engineering, systems engineering, or mathematics.

Special Skills: Creativity, problem-solving abilities, and related experience using 3-D graphics, C or C++ programming, or Java. Written and verbal communication skills are important. Security clearance may be required.

Earn It!
The median annual salary is $94,180.
(Source: U.S. Department of Labor)

As a simulation designer assigned to create a simulation of a typical day in high school, how could you make it as realistic as possible?

. . . MAKE IT REAL!

Use a storyboard approach to planning and describing the various elements you would include in your simulation. You can find storyboard templates by using a search engine to find "storyboard templates."

For the sailing simulation project, no development can begin until the lead designer (you) creates a detailed design document, the bible for the project. The document includes detailed information about every aspect of the project: its look and feel, specific learning objectives and how mastery will be measured, content (including scenarios and dialogue, if any), learning modules, integration of the simulation and actual practice, and technical programming plans.

This is a team effort, as is any simulation project. In creating the design document, you get guidance from the client manager, the person who best understands the goals and preferences of the organization that hired you. You encourage the other designers, the audio and visual artists, and the programmers to provide input as well.

You have to learn a lot about sailing to write the content and learning objectives. Using a variety of resources, you become somewhat knowledgeable about the theory, skills, and techniques of sailing, as well as the effects of wind, waves, and other factors. You also bring in a subject matter expert to ensure that the content in the simulation is correct and complete, a decision you are grateful for many times.

Every simulation project you work on is a new adventure, each presenting different challenges in design, content, and programming. One project may involve game design skills while another may involve using the computer to create simulations or videos. Clients and the people they train with simulations almost always respond with sincere appreciation.

Perhaps the idea of simulations was already brewing when Confucius taught, "I hear and I forget. I see and I remember. I do and I understand."

Social Media Manager

The last place any of your college friends would have expected to find you was in a career in the computer world. In school you were convinced that computers were created solely for the math and science geniuses, people you never understood anyway. You even argued that your constant presence on Facebook, your daily blogging, and your reliance on Twitter "didn't really count" as computer use. Yet here you are, the social media manager for Hudson University, responsible for using Twitter, Facebook, and other interactive media to increase national awareness of the school, attract more applicants, and help create a more diverse community.

Hudson University is an excellent liberal arts school, but not well known beyond its immediate area. While Hudson's administrators want to continue to use traditional media, such as newspapers and TV advertisements, they also realize that such one-way communication cannot really convey the campus' energy and excitement. Your job is to establish two-way relationships with potential students, creating an emotional involvement with the school.

Your typical morning begins with an analysis of the statistics regarding recent visitors to the Web site. You look at how visitors

GET STARTED NOW!

- In School: Writing, any class that requires oral presentations.
- After School: Start your own blog about a hobby or interest, your experiences in the college application process, or anything else that interests you.
- Around Town: List some of the businesses around town or manufacturers of products you use often. See if you can find Twitter accounts or blogs for them.

found your site and how much time they spent on different areas of the site, thinking about changes to the site that might capitalize on this information. You try to respond to questions and comments that have come in through the Web site, blog, or Twitter as quickly as possible. Then you do a little detective work, looking at what other people have been saying about Hudson by visiting the Web sites and blogs maintained by admissions

counselors and other colleges, college advisers, and general interest newspapers and magazines. Because you can't possibly visit every possible Web site every day, you have an RSS feed that provides you with updates from the sites or blogs you want to follow.

To keep Hudson in the news and online searches, you write for the school's admissions blog and Facebook page. Then you leave comments on some of the other blogs you follow, and initiate some conversations and comment on other ongoing ones. No matter what you do, you are always aware that your job is to create an image of Hudson University and to establish relationships with potential students.

Your afternoons are usually devoted to a different type of research. You need to thoroughly understand the college admissions environment and how it works, and to stay on top of all of the tools and trends in the social media world. You can't risk missing out on any developments, especially since 95 percent of all colleges admissions offices are using social media.

Fitting everything into a workday can be a challenge, but you really love this job. And every day you renew your promise to yourself that you will really try not to get too annoyed with the next person who tells you, "It must be great to get paid to play on Facebook all day."

Software Quality Assurance Analyst

When you were a kid did you drive your parents crazy by asking "what if" questions about everything? You know, every time they tried to plan something with you, you had all kinds of "what if" scenarios for every step of the plan. If so, it probably got a bit exasperating for your parents.

Now that you're an adult working in quality assurance, that old habit comes in handy. Your ability to come up with "what ifs" that go beyond the obvious is what has made you such a highly regarded quality assurance professional. You enjoy your career in quality assurance because it allows you to participate in every phase of a software development project (a good thing), and does not require that you to do any programming (another good thing).

Quality assurance is easily confused with quality control. Quality control, testing for flaws or bugs in the product, is usually performed by the development team. Quality assurance, on the other hand, looks at the development process, evaluating each step so that the final product is of high quality, meets required standards, and achieves all of the client's objectives.

You begin each assignment by reviewing and documenting the client's original requirements. You then dissect the development

GET STARTED NOW!

- In School: Math (algebra, geometry, algebra II, pre-calculus), English, computer science.
- After School: Volunteer to help a favorite teacher grade papers to get an idea of what it's like to review materials for accuracy and consistency.
- Around Town: Apply the "what if" question to different aspects of your world.

plan, look for inconsistencies, contradictions, or gaps in logic. You make sure every client objective is satisfied, and that all standards are met, those set by the company (such as rules for consistency in coding or security issues) as well as those required by law or industry regulation. Because you were not part of the original development team and were not involved in creating the plan, you can be objective, contributing a fresh eye and a different way of thinking.

As you analyze every step of the development process, you dive into "what if" mode and look for anything that can possibly go wrong. Your job is a challenge, trying to find ways to intentionally make the product fail (while it is easier to fix) before a customer accidentally does so (and loses trust in everything the company produces). You design ways to test the product for many types of users and situations. What if a sophisticated user tries to get past security? What if the on-screen instructions aren't clear to an older, nontechnical user? What if the error messages aren't useful? What if the user gets interrupted? What if the program is not shut down correctly?

Because the software programmers do not perform the tests themselves, your instructions and definitions of success are very detailed. You cannot use measures that depend on the tester's opinion, such as whether a "page loads quickly," or there is an "acceptable error message." Instead, you use criteria that are specific and measurable, such as "Page loads in less than 10 seconds" or "Error message tells user to hit escape key to return to previous page."

By examining the results of all the "what ifs" you can imagine, you help the development team create a product that meets or exceeds the customer's expectation. Happy customers, after all, are the name of the game.

Systems Analyst

Worldwide Bank has just agreed to purchase New Way Bank (both of which are imaginary institutions). Like all institutions, banks are required to submit many types of reports to different government agencies. Worldwide Bank has always complied quickly, accurately, and in detail. The bank's directors are concerned that when the two institutions are combined, the current computer systems will not be able to produce the required reports. You have been hired, on a short-term basis, to help develop a new system to manage the larger business.

Your first step is to hold individual and small group meetings with all the end users to learn how they work and what they need. But wait! Before you do that, you'd better learn something about the banking business. These people are really busy with their regular jobs. They may not have the time, or patience, to explain what, to them, is very basic terminology and procedures.

Now that you have spoken to everyone, you are an expert in the business, its goals, and the function of every department in the organization. Of course, in a very large organization, you would not be the only one doing this. A very large manufacturing company, for example, might need several people to assess a specific business function like accounts receivable or inventory control.

GET STARTED NOW!

- In School: Math, science, computer classes.
- After School: Practice your logic and problem-solving talents with brainteasers. Start at http://brainden.com/logic-puzzles.htm and http://www.edcollins.com/logic.
- Around Town: As you go to local businesses or services, pay attention to the ways they use technology to provide their services and products.

Ready to begin your plan? To be sure that you understand everything about how all of the elements of the business relate to each other, you create data flow diagrams. You also use budgeting software to make sure the cost of the project is where it should be. More often than not, the budget will not allow everyone's fantasies to be fulfilled. Part of your job will be to prioritize the functions that the new system can address.

To configure the new system, you select hardware (considering processor speed, amount of RAM, hard drive space, video card, monitor size, and networking equipment), and software (the operating system and applications that are installed on each system). You know from your interviews that different functional areas will require different types of software. And you know from your data flowcharts that these applications must be able to "talk" to each other.

Of course you will document everything about the new system. You provide new data flow-charts and diagrams that show how the operations will be performed. You document the sequence of processing, how the output will look to the users, and how the system will be programmed and how it will operate. And then you document the technical specifications of the hardware, instructional manuals, and anything else the users might need to know.

Once everyone agrees on the new system, the company's hardware and software specialists take over. Your final task is to work with them on testing every aspect of the new system and to recommend changes where necessary.

Technical Support Specialist

Technical support specialists are the experts who know everything about an organization's hardware, software, and systems. They can save the day for a department manager whose computer refuses to print the presentation needed for a meeting in 10 minutes, help an assistant who cannot remember his newly changed password, and train a new employee who has does not know how to use some of the company's systems.

Technical support specialists fix sick computers. They make "house calls" when circumstances permit. Because they are so knowledgeable about every detail of the hardware and software, they can walk almost anyone through diagnosis and repair by telephone even when they are hundreds of miles from the user.

While technical support specialists need very strong computer skills, their communication and people skills are equally important. They have to remember that what seems simple to a computer professional can feel like a crisis to a nontechnical user, especially when the problem interrupts the user's work or endangers meeting a deadline. Such "crises" can transform even the nicest person in the organization into a raging maniac. The most successful

GET STARTED NOW!

- In School: Computer classes, communications.
- After School: Improve your patience and your communication skills. If your school has a peer-to-peer tutoring program, sign up for it.
- Around Town: Notice your experiences with anyone whose job requires them to help you. Observe salespeople, bus drivers, restaurant servers, etc.

CAREER 411

Search It!
Association of Support Professionals at http://www.asponline.com.

Surf It!
Check out some frustrating calls computer support specialists have received at http://www.rinkworks.com/stupid/cs_stuptech.shtml and and http://www.thenetworkadministrator.com/enduserlang.htm.

Read It!
Learn about troubleshooting for many common personal computer problems at http://www.ex-designz.net/pc_troubleshooting.asp.

Learn It!
Minimum Education: Certification, bachelor's or associate's degree.

Typical Majors: Computer science, computer engineering, or information systems.

Special Skills: Technical proficiency in all hardware and software that a specific organization uses, patience, and calm temperament.

Earn It!
The median annual salary is $46,260.
(Source: U.S. Department of Labor)

support specialists are able to remain calm, patient, understanding, and productive even when the person on the other end of the phone is frantic, angry, or demanding.

For companies whose products are computers or software, support specialists may be hired to serve the company's customers, rather than its employees. Many studies have indicated that customer satisfaction with support services is critical to getting customers' loyalty and continued business.

One way to provide efficient, high-quality service is to create multiple levels within the support group. Such multitier systems usually assign level one (initial support) to the basic customer service calls. At this level, the specialist's first goal is to get a good understanding of the problem. While that sounds easy enough, it can be a real challenge if the customer is very stressed and has no understanding of computer technology. Once again patience and the ability to get to the core of the issue are as important as the ability to solve complex computer issues.

Level one specialists can easily resolve many problems, especially the most common ones that involve basic issues such as resetting a username or password, uninstalling or reinstalling a software application, or verifying proper hardware and software setup. This level of service is generally free of charge to the customer.

IF YOU WERE. . .

As a technical support specialist, your job is to answer questions about your favorite software program or computer game (you pick!). How would you explain the program or game's basic features to a new user?

. . . MAKE IT REAL!

Write a script you could use when providing phone or online support to a new user.

Problems that cannot be easily resolved at this level are referred to level two support specialists. If no one at that level can help, the problem goes to level three, the most senior specialists, who will then embark on a serious research mission. Customer problems that reach level three may actually reveal an overlooked flaw in the software, and the designers or programmers have to develop a patch to fix it.

Companies have a real interest in helping their employees and their customers. Technical support specialists are some of the unrecognized heroes who make that happen.

Technical Writer

CAREER 411

Search It!
The Society for Technical Communication at http://www.stc.org.

Surf It!
Visit PlainLanguage.gov, the Web site created to support simplified writing in government communications, at http://www.plainlanguage.gov.

Read It!
Read interesting "before and after" writing examples at http://www.plainlanguage.gov/examples/before_after/index.cfm.

Learn It!
Minimum Education: Bachelor's degree.

Typical Majors: Communications, journalism, or English. A degree in a technical field such as engineering, medicine, or a science can be useful.

Special Skills: Excellent writing and communication skills, ability to understand complex material and present it clearly, organization, persistence, and attention to detail.

Earn It!
The median annual salary is $63,280.

(Source: U.S. Department of Labor)

Imagine you are the president of a technology company that has just released a new product with a revolutionary operating system. Within a few days of the release the customer support lines are flooded with calls for help. Uh oh! A problem with the hardware or software could be devastating.

When you question the customer support agents, you learn that the system does not have any problems (whew!). The calls have been from users unable to find answers to their questions in the user manual. You soon begin to realize that letting the technical development team write the manual was not the best decision you have ever made.

Professional technical writers, who don't make assumptions about what users already know, are better equipped to write such manuals. The design and development professionals provide information about the product. Writers with relevant education or experience in the field have the advantage of needing less of the designers' time for detailed explanation.

Successful technical writers are able to make complex concepts understandable to nontechnical users. They have a clear and concise writing style, know how to organize the manual for easy reference, and format each page for maximum usability.

GET STARTED NOW!

- In School: Technology, English, writing.
- After School: Join the school journalism staff to get experience in writing.
- Around Town: Volunteer to create a brochure or other written materials for organizations such as a library, fire department, homeless shelter, or your favorite place of worship.

How a technical writer presents information is determined in large part by the nature of the audience that will use it. Documentation intended for other experts to use when revisions or adjustments become necessary may need to be organized and formatted for easy access to information, but technical language and complex theories can be returned. Documentation intended for the technicians who will maintain and repair a product can also retain technical terms, but may require an explanation of some of the underlying theories and decisions.

Instructions and user manuals for nontechnical users can be the most interesting, as well as the most challenging, assignments. The reality is that even the best user manual will be read by few, if any, of the products purchasers. It is more likely that users, feeling annoyed, frustrated, or angry about a problem with the product, will frantically search for the manual and an easy solution to their problem.

A good manual separates the big puzzle into smaller, more manageable pieces. It usually includes a table of contents, a detailed index, labeled illustrations, and a glossary of technical terms. When a concept mentioned in one section is explained in another, a good manual often directs the user to the specific page with the explanation.

It is easy to view a user manual as just an added expense. Although there is a cost to creating such a manual, the greater cost may come from customer service calls, negative product reviews, and harm to the company's image. The best user manuals are so clear and easy to use that it is easy to assume that "anyone" can do it. As you learned from the introduction of your new operating system, good technical writing is a specialized skill, and should be left to the professionals.

3-D Computer Animator

If you want to be a 3-D computer animator you must A) be a creative thinker, draw well, and love 3-D animated films and games or B) be really good at math and science. The answer? Both A and B! Are you surprised? Read on to find out why.

Animation, the process of making still objects appear to move, is achieved by creating a series of very similar images, each containing small changes in areas that will appear to move. When these images are presented in sequence, with each image quickly replacing the one before it, our brains blend the small changes together and we perceive motion.

Before computers, each image in an animation was hand-drawn on a transparent sheet called a cel. It took a lot of cels to make a film: 23 cels for just one second of film and almost 84,000 cels for an hour. Whew!

Computers are the key to 3-D effects that were not possible in earlier times. Three-dimensional art makes objects on a flat screen appear to be solid and to exist in space that is in front of or behind other objects. Painters have used perspective, color, light, and shading to create the impression of three dimensions for hundreds of years. Computer artists use those same techniques, applying them in a different way.

GET STARTED NOW!!

- In School: Focus on algebra, geometry, trigonometry, calculus, design, computer graphics.
- After School: Practice animation with free software, such as Blender 3D. You can find many free tutorials for it online.
- Around Town: Be a people watcher. Notice how they move and convey mood and emotion. Sketch your observations in a notebook.

CAREER 411

Search It!
Animation World Magazine at http://www.awn.com/magazines/animation-world-magazine.

Surf It!
Create animated avatars at http://www.evolver.com or learn from professionals at http://www.animationtipsandtricks.com.

Read It!
Find out how 3-D animation works at http://www.howstuffworks.com/3dgraphics.htm and http://entertainment.howstuffworks.com/computer-animation.htm.

Learn It!
Minimum Education: Bachelor's degree. Associate's degree sometimes acceptable.

Typical Majors: For technical positions: engineering, math, physics, computer science. For other positions: computer animation, media, fine arts.

Special Skills: Creative thinking, adaptability, organization, ability to work as part of a team, attention to detail, patience, expertise with current animation software.

Earn It!
The median annual salary ranges from $40,000 to $60,000, depending on industry.
(Source: U.S. Department of Labor)

Painters work with sections of an image, applying color with a brush or other tool. Computer artists work with pixels (picture elements), the very smallest units in an image. To create the algorithms, or rules, that tell computers the color to assign to each pixel, they use calculus, trigonometry, linear algebra, and other math. Animators use the principles of physics, anatomy, and other sciences to maintain the realism created by the 3-D graphics, making sure that every movement is natural, logical, and possible in the real world.

When animators create new characters, they usually begin by creating a video (or representation) that demonstrates a range of facial expressions and movements. Using their representations as guides, artists create rough drawings of their characters and load them into their computers. Eventually the artists add digital "strings" like those used to manipulate puppets. Other, less technical animators "pull" those strings to animate the character.

Computers then render each frame, combining all the digital information, for characters, lighting, colors, props, and other components into a visual display. Although the computers are very fast (e.g., Pixar uses 100 supercomputers that perform 400 billion calculations per second), it still takes six days to produce one

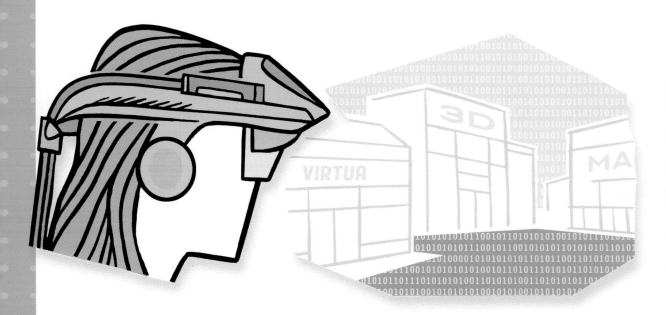

second of film. Animators sometimes find fulfilling the visions of directors and screenwriters challenging. Before *Finding Nemo*, no one had ever successfully portrayed animated water. *The Incredibles* was the first time animators ever created the illusion of fabric blowing in the wind. Both of these accomplishments are a tribute to the creativity of 3-D animators. It is hard to imagine what effects they will achieve next.

Usability Specialist

Sometimes it's the little things in life that make people happy. Have you ever pounded on the bottom of a ketchup bottle, trying to get just enough to spice up your burger but ending up with a small ocean of ketchup instead? If so, you were probably really happy when some manufacturers redesigned bottles by turning them upside down so that the ketchup could glide out in whatever quantity you wanted.

Usability, the ease of using a product, is especially important in Web site design. When a site is confusing or difficult to navigate, users do not make purchases or return to the site. Usability specialists are the experts who combine technology and psychology to make a site pleasurable for the user and productive for the organization that created it.

Let's say that you are a usability specialist, and that your newest client is a well-known shoe company. The company's Web site attracts a lot of visitors, but they spend very little time on the site and sales are very low. Your task is to make the Web site more profitable.

As an experienced usability specialist, you know that a common challenge for retail sites is the ability for users to

GET STARTED NOW!

- In School: Graphic design, writing, psychology, and communications.
- After School: Keep a journal listing the Web sites you visit for homework and for entertainment. Keep track of any features that make the site especially enjoyable or difficult to use.
- Around Town: Visit the Web sites of some of your favorite local businesses and see how user-friendly they are.

search by different attributes. For the shoe company, customers should be able to search for a desired style, color, size, price, or any combination of the above. They should be able to use regional names for a style, getting the same results whether they search for deck shoes, boat shoes, or topsiders. If the search is confusing, or takes too much time, energy, or effort, the customer is more likely to leave the site than to struggle through it.

The basic guidelines for user-friendly Web sites are the result of several types of research. In some studies, researchers watched users navigate through the site, noting where they encountered problems or frustrations. Other studies involved professionally designed interviews, either in a group setting or online. Some studies have even used a machine that can track the user's eye movements and identify the parts of each screen that attract the most attention.

Previous research is a guide, but usability specialists still test their designs with people similar to those the site is targeted toward. Results vary depending on the characteristics of the users (such as age and gender), the purpose of the site (such as information, sales, or fun), and even the colors and illustrations.

Some usability specialists work on all aspects of a project. Some specialize in research, and others develop or test alternatives to low-scoring pages. As smart phones replace computers for many customers, some specialists are developing expertise to accommodate the ways that technology differs from Web site technology.

Usability specialists recognize that whether the product is a ketchup bottle, a microwave oven, a college application, or a retail Web site, the user's positive experience will always be a major factor in that product's success.

Video Game Designer

Some people love video games. Other lucky people get paid to design them. Designing a game is a long, detail-oriented process, requiring creativity, technical expertise, and patience.

Let's say you are a game designer, with a great idea for a new game. Although you will have overall responsibility for the game, the rest of the development team has to understand your vision also. You begin by writing out the major features of the game: the setting, plot, and rules. To be sure everything is clear, you include drawings, flowcharts, and diagrams. This information is the beginning of the design document, the ultimate how-to guide for the production of your game. Details about characters, plot twists, and clues are added as decisions are made. As the game develops, you may change features based on level of difficulty and logic, remembering to put everything in the design document.

Video games are created by development teams, which can range from one or two people to several hundred, depending on the game's complexity. Large teams include designers, writers, graphic artists, sound designers, and programmers. Often there are subspecialties within these positions. Level designers, those

GET STARTED NOW!

- In School: Computer programming, art, design, writing.
- After School: Play games! Experiment with those games that allow you to modify them or create new levels. Try games in categories other than your favorites.
- Around Town: Keep a notebook and enter your game ideas, no matter how strange they may seem at the time. Anything (or anyone) can be inspiration for a character or plot someday.

CAREER 411

Search It!
Entertainment Software Association at http://www.theesa.com.

Surf It!
Check out the winners of the Serious Games Challenge at http://www.sgschallenge.com.

Read It!
Compare different styles of games at http://www.seriousgamessource.com and http://www.casualconnect.org.

Learn It!
Minimum Education: Bachelor's degree.

Typical Majors: English, creative writing, video game design, or video game programming.

Special Skills: Organized, familiar with gaming and computer science, creativity, problem-solving abilities, strong written and verbal communication skills, and the ability to work on a team.

Earn It!
The mean annual wage is $50,3000.

(Source: U.S. Department of Labor)

responsible for the layout and details of each level in the game, for first-person shooter (FPS) games use different skills from those needed by role-playing or massively multiplayer online (MMO) games.

No matter what type of game you most enjoy playing, keep your options open by exploring the opportunities and financial rewards offered by other types of games.

By 2010 so many people were also playing games on mobile phones, iPads, and other devices that the greatest demand was for casual games, those that a single player can learn quickly and play in a short period of time. Solitaire and Minesweeper are examples of early casual games. Social games, like Scrabble, are similar, but allow many people to play at once.

The most profitable games are the social network games that appear on sites such as Facebook. Zynga, (the company that created FarmVille), achieved revenues of $500 million a year, only three years after its founding. The most impressive games are the complex, MMO role-playing games, such as World of Warcraft.

Video games are no longer just for amusement. Developers now create serious games that allow users to experience situations that would be impossible to create in the real world. Games for military training, surgical techniques, and disaster preparedness are critical in training people to be confident in actual situations.

Whatever you choose as your specialty, remember that personal skills are just as important as technical ones. The stars in this field are people who are creative, able to adjust as technology and customers' interests change, good problem solvers, and excellent team players.

Video Game Sound Designer

Before a new video game is released, it is usually tested by experienced game players. If those first players report that they felt as if they were actually living in the world of the game, or that they became so involved that they totally lost track of time, it's a pretty sure bet that the game will be a big success.

Of the many factors that contribute to intense player involvement, sound is one that is often overlooked. Sound designers have major impact on making the game's world "real" by modifying the sound qualities of dialogue, adding sound effects, and using music effectively.

Beyond enhancing the game's world, sound also minimizes real-world distractions that might interfere with the player's involvement. The creators of the earliest video games understood this principle. Back then, the capacity for data storage was limited and there was no way to convert digital information to recognizable sound waves, so sound was limited to a few annoying beeps and blips. With modern sound cards and other technology, games can use realistic sounds, interactive music that changes based on the player's actions, and 3-D positional audio that makes sound

GET STARTED NOW!

- In School: Computer science, math, music, and English.
- After School: Learn to play a musical instrument, sing in the school chorus, and/or join the marching band.
- Around Town: Play video games and pay attention to the sounds you hear. Can you figure out how some of them are made?

seem to come from the direction that an on-screen avatar might hear it.

One way to make the game's world more believable is through ambient, or background, sound. A certain mix of sounds instantly makes us feel that we are in a hospital, on a battlefield, or in an office. Other sounds tell us about offscreen settings: that there is a factory beyond the office's door, that we are on a street with heavy traffic, or that a storm is raging outside.

As ambient sound sets the scene, special sound effects make actions more real. Imagine, for example, a scene in which your avatar gets into a parked car and drives off...in silence. Now imagine the same scene, but add the sounds of a key turning in the ignition lock, the engine revving, and the tires squealing. Which image is more real or engaging?

One secret of successful sound effects is that real sounds do not always *feel* realistic. The actual sound of a breaking bone, for example, is not very dramatic. The snap of crisp celery is a lot closer to the way we think the break should sound. If the sounds in the game are not what the player expects them to be, his involvement in the game's world is diminished.

The most specialized creators of sound effects are the Foley (meaning sound effects for film) artists. They are extremely creative and resourceful, producing sounds for actions we know well, for sounds that may not exist in reality (such as robots tearing each other apart), or for sounds that have never been heard by anyone (such as a bullet piercing a skull).

The best sound design in the world will probably not make a poor product good. But sound designers know that without their contribution, many great games might have been just okay.

Even though the average gamer will probably take your hard work for granted, the game development team and other sound designers will recognize how much you contribute to the final product. And you'll know that every footstep, crash, punch, kiss, or giggle you add makes the game more playable and enjoyable.

Webmaster

Your dear Aunt Sally owns a popular bakery. Everyone loves the products at *her* bakery. She heard about a bakery in Chicago that is making a fortune selling goodies through its Web site. Now Aunt Sally wants her own Web site and she happens to know that you just finished a degree in Web design. She offers you a deal you can't refuse (sweetened with the promise of a lifetime supply of cupcakes), so you agree.

You definitely have the skills for this project. You know the software commonly used for Web sites (HTML, CSS, C++, or Java); you understand computer operating systems, search engines, and databases; and you created a terrific portfolio in your design classes at school.

Although the Webmaster job can be defined in many different ways, in this case it is the person responsible for creating and managing everything about Aunt Sally's Web site. "Everything" includes design, development, marketing, maintenance, and content, in addition to writing the actual code. It is a lot to do but, if funds permit, you may bring in a designer or programmer to help.

To get the site started, you register its domain name, then set up a merchant account (so customers can use credit cards), select a shopping cart program (to collect the information needed to ship product), and install an SSL (secure sockets layer, for privacy). You

CAREER 411

Search It!
WebProfessionals.org at http://webprofessionals.org.

Surf It!
See which Web sites the professionals in the industry selected for the Webby Awards at http://www.webbyawards.com.

Read It!
Visit the Web Developer's Virtual Library at http://www.wdvl.com.

Learn It!
Minimum Education: Bachelor's degree, certification, or on-the-job training.

Typical Majors: Graphic design, Web design.

Special Skills: Understanding of computer operating systems, computer graphics, search engines, and Internet standards. Experience in Web site development, creative, and excellent communication skills.

Earn It!
The median annual salary is $69,160.
(Source: U.S. Department of Labor)

GET STARTED NOW!

- In School: Computer science, math, writing, art, graphic design.
- After School: Volunteer to help keep your school's Web site up-to-date.
- Around Town: Every time you visit a new local store or restaurant, go online and see if they have an easy-to-find and easy-to-use Web site.

also make sure the site meets all legal requirements, including copyright and privacy statements.

In the actual design of the site, elements such as color and layout obviously have a strong influence on how customers view the company. Other elements have a more subtle influence. For example, customers will leave without purchasing if navigation is complicated, ordering instructions are complex, or menus, links, or text are confusing.

Aunt Sally knows that she has to get people to visit her site in order to sell her products and earn money. She has already discovered that Google searches for "online bakery" and "gourmet bakery" yield links to more than a million Web sites. Aunt Sally is very clear: She does not want to be at the end of that list. In fact, she does not want to be past the first few pages.

The order of the sites on Google results is not random. Webmasters know that complying with the Web Standards Project and following the suggestions from Google's Webmaster Guidelines are two of the ways to stay out of the bottom of the search engine barrel.

Even when the site is completed and online, you are not quite off the hook. You continue to check the navigation and links daily, fixing any problems you find, and responding to all customer comments. Updates (and cupcakes!) are a regularly scheduled event.

EXPERIMENT WITH SUCCESS

Stop! Hold it right there. You are so not ready to experiment with success until you have explored your way to a career idea that makes you wonder, "Is this one right for me?"

You will know you are ready to take things to the next level when you are still curious about a specific career idea even after you have used the tools featured in Section Two to:

- Investigate that career idea so thoroughly that you know almost as much about what it's like as someone who is already doing it
- Complete a Hire Yourself activity with impressive results

If, after all that, you still want to know more, this section is where you can crank things up by:

- Talking with people who already have careers like the one you want
- Looking at different types of employment situations where people get paid to do what you want to do
- Figuring out a few next steps for getting from where you are now (high school) to where you want to go (a successful career)

In other words, you are going to:

- ASK for advice and start building a career-boosting network
- ASSESS a variety of workplace options
- ADDRESS options to make the most of now to get ready for a successful future

ASK for Advice and Start Building a Career-Boosting Network

There's nothing like going straight to the source to find out what a specific career is really like. After all, who's more likely to have the inside scoop on the real deal than someone who has actually "been there, done that." It is surprisingly easy to get most people talking about their careers. All you have to do is ask.

E-mail, Twitter, Facebook, and other cool social networking tools now make it easier than ever to touch base with almost any expert in the world for advice and information. But whether you conduct your career chats the old-fashioned way with face-to-face conversations or via the latest and greatest technologies, the following tips will help you make a good first impression.

1 **Practice with people you already know.** Start asking parents, relatives, neighbors, and other trusted adults to talk about what their work is really like, and you're likely to be amazed by what you find out.

ROAD TRIP, ANYONE?

Listen in on the fascinating discoveries made by students participating in the Road Trip Nation project, an organization that "sends people on the road who are interested in exploring the world outside their comfort zone, talking with individuals who chose to define their own road in life, and sharing their experiences with our generation." Hear their stories and interviews online at http://roadtripnation. com or tune in to an online episode of the PBS series, *Road Trip Nation*, at http://www.pbs.org/wnet/roadtripnation/episodes.html.

2 **Think about what you want to know before you start asking questions.** Jot down a few questions that you can refer to if you get nervous or the conversation starts to lag. Keep the conversation flowing by asking open-ended questions that require more than simple yes or no answers like:

- Tell me about…
- How do you feel about…?
- What was it like…?

3 **Be polite, professional, and considerate of the person's time.** In other words, don't be a pest! Just because you can access any person, any place, any time doesn't mean that you should.

4 **Seek answers *and* advice.** Make the most of any opportunity to learn from other people's successes and mistakes. Be sure to ask them what they know now that they wish they had known when they were your age.

You may want to add some of these questions to your interviews:

- How do your childhood interests relate to your choice of career path?
- How did you first learn about the job you have today?
- In what ways is your job different from how you expected it to be?
- What is a typical day on the job like for you?
- What are the best and worst parts of your job?

- If anything were possible, how would you change your job description?
- What kinds of people do you usually meet in your work?
- How is your product made (or service delivered)?
- What other kinds of professionals work here?
- Tell me about the changes you have seen in your industry over the years. What do you see as the future of the industry?

5 **Keep your career-information network growing.**
Conclude each interview with a sincere thank you and a request for recommendations about other people or resources to turn to for additional information.

CAREER CHATS

Think about who knows what you want to know. Use online news and professional association Web sites to identify experts in your field of interest. For extra help finding contact information, use Google to identify the person's company Web site or other professional affiliations. And, of course, do make use of the time-honored "friend of a friend of a friend" network to find contacts known to friends, parents, neighbors, teachers, and others who share an interest in helping you succeed.

Depending on each person's availability, interviews can be arranged onsite at a person's place of employment (with parental permission and supervision only), via a prescheduled phone conversation, or online with e-mail, Skype, or other social networking tools. Find out which method is most convenient for the person you'd like to interview.

One note of encouragement (and caution) before you get started. Most people are more than happy to talk about their careers. After all, who doesn't like talking about themselves? So, on the one hand, you don't have to worry about asking since most people will say yes if they have the time. On the other hand, you'll want to be careful about who you contact. Take every precaution to make sure that every person is legit (as opposed to being certified creepers) and make sure that a trusted adult (such as a parent or teacher) has your back as you venture out into the real world.

With that said, use the following chart (or, if this book does not belong to you, create one like it) to keep track of whom you contact and what they say. Once you get the hang of it, use the same process to contact others who are likely to know what you need to know about your future career.

Contact Information

Name: _____

Company: _____

Title: _____

Company Web Site: _____

Preferred Contact Method: _____

❏ Phone _____

❏ E-mail _____

❏ Twitter _____

❏ Facebook _____

❏ Blog _____

❏ Other _____

CONTACT LOG		
Date/Time	**Question**	**Answer**

Lessons Learned

Nice as it is to talk to other people about their success, there's a point where you can't help but wonder what it all means for you. Here's your chance to apply what you've learned from your career chats to your own situation. Take a few minutes to think through your best answers to the following questions:

- What do you know about this career that you didn't know before?
- What kind of knowledge and skills do you need to acquire to prepare for a career like this?
- Are you more or less inclined to pursue this type of career? Why or why not?

ASSESS a Variety of Workplace Options

Employers come in all shapes and sizes. They run the gamut from huge multinational conglomerates to small mom-and-pop shops with a lot of options in-between. Big or small, before any employer agrees to hire you, they are going to want to know pretty much everything there is to know about you. Where did you go to school? What kind of grades did you make? What are your professional goals? Questions like these will keep flying until an employer is absolutely certain that you are the right choice for their company.

But guess what? It takes two to create a mutually beneficial employment relationship—an employer who gets what he needs and an employee who gets what he wants. In other words, that get-acquainted curiosity cuts both ways. It's just as important for you to find out if the company is a good fit for you as it is for them. After all, your success is their success and vice versa.

In most cases it's a bit early to decide on your ultimate employer with any precision. However, it's the perfect time to take a look at the options. Can you see yourself in the fast-paced world of a high-powered Fortune 500 firm? Are you better suited for an energetic, entrepreneurial, start-up company? Would you just as soon shuck the corporate world for a job that lets you work outdoors or, perhaps, one that requires a lot of travel?

Figuring out what kind of environment you want to work in is almost as important as figuring out what you want to do. Fortunately the Internet makes scouting out workplace options just a few mouse clicks away. Use the following tips to find out more about employers who hire people to do the kind of work you want to do.

- **Surf the Web** to seek out companies according to industry, career type, or geographic location. For instance, a quick Google search for "agribusiness" is likely to yield a list of resources that includes the U.S. Department of Agriculture to companies specializing in everything from beverages and beehives to snack foods and seeds.

- **Find a List** that meets some sort of criteria. Want to work for one of the nation's biggest, most successful companies? Run a search for Fortune 500 companies at http://www. forbes.com. Want to find an exciting, up-and-coming company? Look for a list of "fastest growing companies" at http://www.inc.com or http://money.cnn.com. Want to find a company that treats its employees especially well? Track down a list of great places to work at http://www. greatplacestowork.com. Prefer a family-friendly company? Check out Working Mother's lists of bests at http://www. workingmother.com/best-companies.
- **Visit Company Web Sites** to compare opportunities associated with different kinds of employment situations—government, corporate, and small business, for instance. Simply run a search for the name of any company you want to know about—even most small companies have a Web site these days. Be sure to check out the current "careers" or "job listings" sections to get a sense of what the company looks for and offers prospective employees. Also use the Google news feature to look for current newsworthy articles about a prospective employer.

How a company presents itself online offers an interesting perspective of what the company's culture might be like. These types of online resources also offer a great way to find out more about a company's products and services, mission, values, clients, and reputation. The bonus is all the contact names and details you can use to seek out additional information.

Employer Profiles

Ready for a little cyber-snooping? Go online to track down information about three different types of employers: **a major corporation** (think Fortune 500); **a small business** (think entrepreneurial); and **a government agency** (think local, state, or federal) that offers opportunities associated with the career pathway you'd like to pursue. Use the following chart to record your discoveries and compare the results.

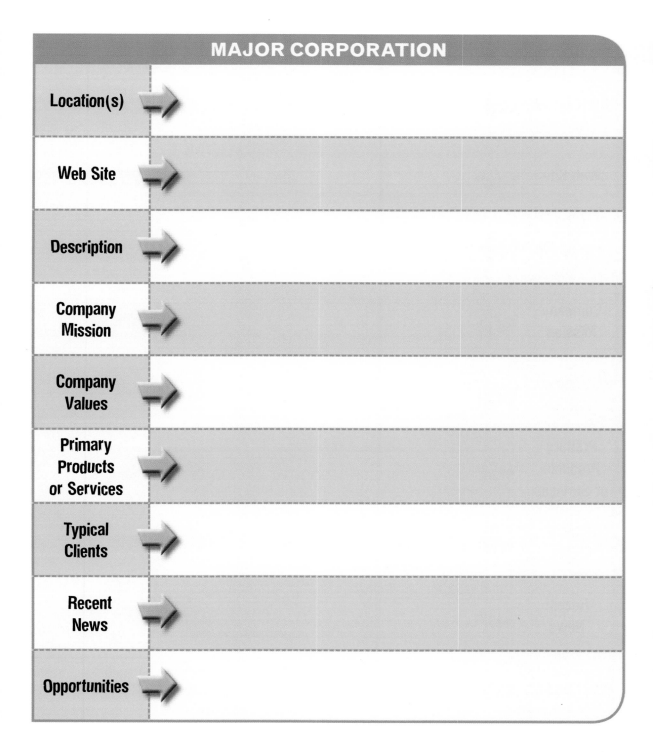

MAJOR CORPORATION

Location(s)	
Web Site	
Description	
Company Mission	
Company Values	
Primary Products or Services	
Typical Clients	
Recent News	
Opportunities	

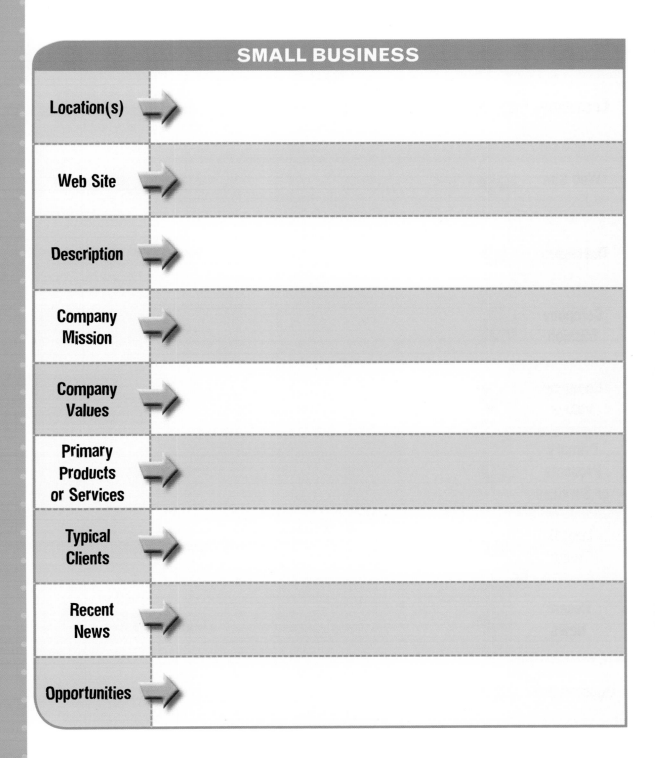

SMALL BUSINESS

Location(s)

Web Site

Description

Company Mission

Company Values

Primary Products or Services

Typical Clients

Recent News

Opportunities

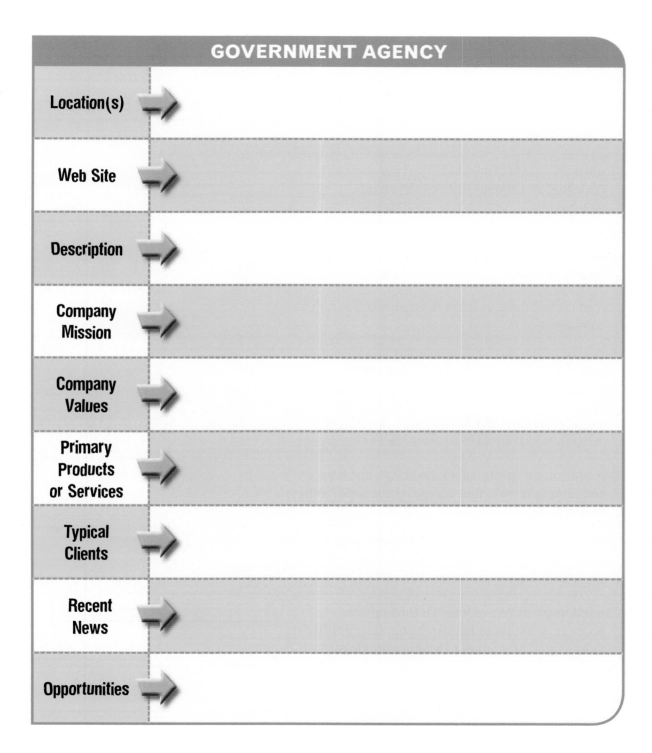

GOVERNMENT AGENCY

Location(s)

Web Site

Description

Company Mission

Company Values

Primary Products or Services

Typical Clients

Recent News

Opportunities

Lessons Learned

Take time out to think through what you've learned about your workplace preferences. Use the following chart to compare the pros and cons of each situation and apply what you learned to what you want in a future work environment.

	Major Corporation
Based on your first impression of the company's Web site, how would you describe each employer?	
What factor(s) did you find most appealing about each company? (Size, geographic location, opportunities for advancement, etc.)	
What factor(s) did you like least about the company?	
What (if any) types of employment opportunities interested you most at each company?	
In what ways does (or doesn't) the company's mission statement and values align with what matters most to you in a future career?	
Would you be comfortable devoting your time and talents to help this company succeed? Why or why not?	
If you had to choose between these three types of employers, which type would you expect to enjoy working for the most? Why?	
Based on what you've learned through this process, what three factors have you identified as essential attributes of a future employer?	1 _____ 2 _____ 3 _____

Small Business	Government Agency
1 _____	1 _____
2 _____	2 _____
3 _____	3 _____

ADDRESS Options to Make the Most of Now

Well—big sigh of relief—you've almost made it through the entire Discover, Explore, Experiment process. This time and effort represent a huge investment in your future and has introduced a process you can rely on to guide you through a lifetime of career decisions.

But, you may well be wondering: "How do I get from here to there?"

Good question.

The answer? One step at a time.

No matter if you are moving full steam ahead toward a particular career or still meandering through the options—even if you are freaking out with indecision—here's what to do next: Map out a plan!

Your plan does not have to be set in stone with no wiggle room to take advantage of new opportunities. Instead it should move you forward along the pathway you choose to pursue and provide solid tools that prepare you to make the most of every opportunity that comes your way.

The first approach is complicated and, face it, a bit unrealistic. After all, who knows how your interests and talents will evolve over time? It's impossible to predict what kinds of as-yet-unheard-of opportunities will emerge in the future. Think about it. Did your great-grandparents dream of becoming computer programmers or Webmasters? Probably not. Chances are personal computers were an unimaginable innovation when they were making career choices. Long story short, the perfect career for you may not even exist yet.

The second approach is simple and leaves plenty of room for change as life and experience present new opportunities. It's not an attempt to plot out every last detail of your entire life. Instead, focus on making the most of now. What can you do now to get ready for a successful future? How can you get out of "stuck mode" and inch just a little closer to some actual choices?

The first thing you can do is to make the most of the opportunities waiting right under your nose for you to find them. These opportunities include wonderful new high school options designed to help students like you connect academic learning to real-world opportunities. Career academies, career pathways, career and technical education opportunities, and early college programs are just a few ways you can make the most of now.

Joining after-school clubs, volunteering for a cause you care about, and even getting a part-time job are other ways you can expand your horizons and gain useful experience. If it's information you are after, why not try some job shadowing or an internship at a local company of interest? Of course it goes without saying that getting good grades and staying out of trouble are helpful strategies, too.

There is so much you can do today to prepare for a brighter future. So why are you still sitting there? Start researching the options so you can map out a few next steps to get you where you want to go.

Next Step Options

X marks the spot. You are here in high school. How do you get from high school to a successful career? Find out all you can about various options offered at your school or in your community. Use the following checklist of options to keep track of details about each opportunity. You'll get a chance to map out specific next steps later.

OPTIONS

What kinds of career academies, career pathways, career and technical education, early college, or other special academic and career readiness programs does your school offer that fit with your career aspirations?

Ask your school adviser or guidance counselor to help you sort out which options are right for you.

What kinds of core academic courses can you take to prepare for a specific career pathway?

For instance, advanced math and science courses are good choices for someone looking toward a career in engineering.

What kinds of electives can you fit into your schedule to explore different kinds of opportunities?

For instance, environmental studies is a good choice for someone considering a green career.

What clubs and after-school activities provide opportunities to explore various career interests?

For instance, 4-H for someone interested in agriculture or natural resources; science competitions for future scientists; Future Business Leaders of America for business wannabes.

What local businesses offer opportunities for firsthand observations of how people do what you want to do?

Ask your school adviser or guidance counselor about job shadowing opportunities. Or go online to http://www.jobshadow.com to find out about local job shadowing opportunities.

What kinds of internship opportunities are available for students to get real-world work experiences?

Talk to your school adviser or guidance counselor about internship opportunities at your school.

Where can you volunteer to help further a favorite cause while, at the same time, building useful skills and experience?

Talk with the leader of a favorite community or religious organization about volunteer opportunities or go online to explore service learning options at http://www.learnandserve.gov.

What does your high school do to introduce students to various college, military, and other career training programs?

Ask your school adviser or guidance counselor for a schedule of college visits, career fairs, and other resources.

YOUR CHOICES

Academic and Career Readiness Programs

Core Academic Courses

Elective Courses

Clubs and After-School Activities

Job Shadowing Opportunities

Internships

Volunteer Experiences

College and Career Training Programs

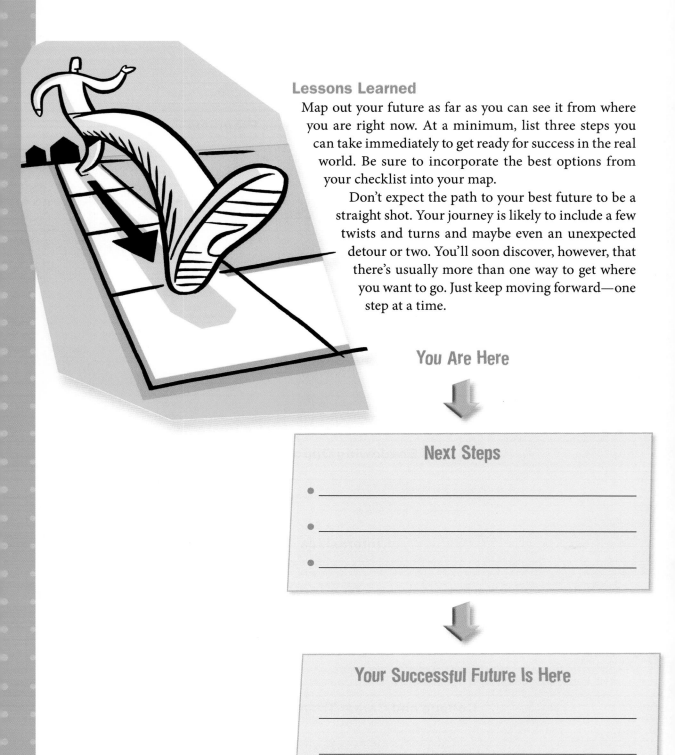

Lessons Learned

Map out your future as far as you can see it from where you are right now. At a minimum, list three steps you can take immediately to get ready for success in the real world. Be sure to incorporate the best options from your checklist into your map.

Don't expect the path to your best future to be a straight shot. Your journey is likely to include a few twists and turns and maybe even an unexpected detour or two. You'll soon discover, however, that there's usually more than one way to get where you want to go. Just keep moving forward—one step at a time.

You Are Here

Next Steps

- _____
- _____
- _____

Your Successful Future Is Here

_____

_____

A Final Word

Take a look back at all you've accomplished as you've worked your way through this book.

- You made important discoveries about yourself and the world of work.
- You explored a wide variety of career ideas found along this career pathway.
- You've experimented with three success strategies.

At this point, you may or may not be satisfied that you've got your future all figured out. Chances are you still aren't quite sure. Chances are even greater that things will change (maybe even more than once) before you put your big plans into action. After all, who knows what you'll discover as you get out there and experience the real world in new and interesting ways.

One thing is certain though: You are in better shape now than you were when you started reading this book. Why? Because you now have tools you can use to make well-informed career decisions—as you take your first steps toward your future career and throughout your life as you pursue new opportunities.

You've been wrestling with three big questions throughout this book.

- What do you know a lot about?
- What are you really good at doing?
- Where can you put that knowledge and those skills to work?

Rely on these questions to point you toward new opportunities as you move along your career path. Adjust them to reflect your constantly evolving experience and expertise, of course. And, whenever you find yourself in need of a career compass, simply revisit those questions again.

Then update that knowledge, hone those skills, and look for an employer who is willing to pay you to do what you really want to do!

With all this said and done, there's just one more question to ask: What *are* you going to do when you graduate?

Appendix

CAREER IDEAS FOR TEENS SERIES

Find out more about the world of work in any of these *Career Ideas for Teens* titles:

- *Agriculture, Food, and Natural Resources*
- *Architecture and Construction*
- *Arts and Communications*
- *Business, Management, and Administration*
- *Education and Training*
- *Finance*
- *Government and Public Service*
- *Health Science*
- *Hospitality and Tourism*
- *Human Services*
- *Information Technology*
- *Law and Public Safety*
- *Manufacturing*
- *Marketing*
- *Science, Technology, Engineering, and Math*
- *Transportation, Distribution, and Logistics*

VIRTUAL SUPPORT TEAM

As you continue your quest to determine just what it is you want to do with your life, you'll find that you are not alone. There are many people and organizations who want to help you succeed. Here are two words of advice: let them! Take advantage of all the wonderful resources so readily available to you.

The first place to start is your school's guidance center. There you will probably find a variety of free resources which include information about careers, colleges, and other types of training opportunities; details about interesting events, job shadowing activities, and internship options; and access to useful career assessment tools.

In addition, there's a world of information just a mouse click away—use it! The following Internet resources provide all kinds of information and ideas that can help you find your future.

MAKE AN INFORMED CHOICE

Following are three especially useful career Web sites. Be sure to bookmark and visit them often as you consider various career options.

America's Career InfoNet

http://www.acinet.org

Quite possibly the most comprehensive source of career exploration anywhere, this U.S. Department of Labor Web site includes all kinds of current information about wages, market conditions, employers, and employment trends. Make sure to visit the site's career video library where you'll find links to more than 450 videos featuring real people doing real jobs.

Careers & Colleges

http://www.careersandcolleges.com

Here you'll find useful information about college, majors, scholarships, and other training options.

Career OneStop–Students and Career Advisors

http://www.careeronestop.org/studentsandcareeradvisors/
  studentsandcareeradvisors.aspx

This Web site is brought to you compliments of the U.S. Department of Labor, Employment and Training Administration, and is designed especially for students like you. Here you'll find information on occupations and industries, internships, schools, and more.

GET A JOB

Whether you're curious about the kinds of jobs currently in big demand or you're actually looking for a job, the following Web sites are a great place to do some virtual job-hunting:

America's Job Bank

http://www.ajb.org

Another example of your (or, more accurately, your parents') tax dollars at work, this well-organized Web site is sponsored by the U.S. Department of Labor. Job seekers can post résumés and use the site's search engines to search through more than a million job listings by location or by job type.

Monster.com

http://www.monster.com

One of the Internet's most widely used employment Web sites, this is where you can search for specific types of jobs in specific parts of the country, network with millions of people, and find useful career advice.

Career Builder

http://www.careerbuilder.com

Another mega-career Web site where you can find out more about what employers are looking for in employees and get a better idea about in-demand professions.

EXPLORE BY CAREER PATHWAY

An especially effective way to explore career options is to look at careers associated with a personal interest or fascination with a certain type of industry. The following Web sites help you narrow down your options in a focused way:

All Career Clusters

Careership

http://mappingyourfuture.org/planyourcareer/careership

Find careers related to any of the 16 career clusters by clicking on the "Review Careers by Cluster" icon.

Agriculture, Food, and Natural Resources

Agrow Knowledge

http://www.agrowknow.org/

Grow your knowledge about this career pathway at the National Resource Center for Agriscience and Technology Education Web site.

Architecture and Construction

Construct My Future

http://www.constructmyfuture.com

With more than $600 billion annually devoted to new construction projects, about 6 million Americans build careers in this industry. This Web site, sponsored by the Association of Equipment Distributors Foundation, Association of Equipment Manufacturers, and Associated General Contractors, introduces an interesting array of construction-related professions.

Make It Happen

http://www.buildingcareers.org

Another informative construction-related Web site—this one sponsored by the Home Builders Institute.

Arts and Communications

My Arts Career

http://www.myartscareer.org

Find out how to put your artistic talents to work at this Web site sponsored by the Center for Arts Education.

Business, Management, and Administration

Careers in Business

http://www.careers-in-business.com

Find links to help you get down to the business of finding a career in business.

Education and Training

Careership

http://mappingyourfuture.org/planyourcareer/careership

Find careers related to education, training, and library by clicking on the "Review Careers by Cluster" icon.

Finance

Careers in Finance

http://www.careers-in-finance.com/

Find a wide variety of links related to careers in finance.

Government and Public Service

Public Service Careers

http://www.publicservicecareers.org

This authoritative Web site is cohosted by the National Association of Schools of Public Affairs and Administration and the American Society for Public Administration.

Health Science

Campaign for Nursing Future

http://campaignfornursing.com/nursing-careers

Here's where to find information on nursing careers from A–Z.

Discover Nursing

http://www.discovernursing.com

More helpful information on nursing opportunities for men, women, minorities, and people with disabilities brought to you by Johnson & Johnson.

Explore Health Careers

http://explorehealthcareers.org/en/Field/1/Allied_Health
_Professions

Find out about nearly 200 allied health careers at this informative Web site.

Hospitality and Tourism

O*Net Hospitality and Tourism Career Cluster

http://online.onetcenter.org/find/career?c=9

Visit this useful Web site to see career profiles about a wide variety of hospitality and tourism positions.

Human Services

Health and Human Services

http://www.hhs.gov

Explore federal health and human services opportunities associated with the U.S. Department of Health and Human Services.

Information Technology

Pathways to Technology

http://www.pathwaystotechnology.org/index.html

Find ideas and information about careers associated with all kinds of state-of-the-art and emerging technologies.

Law and Public Safety

National Partnership for Careers in Law, Public Safety, Corrections and Security

http://www.ncn-npcpss.com/

Initially established with funding from the U.S. Department of Justice, this organization partners with local and federal public safety agencies, secondary and postsecondary education institutions, and an array of professional and educational associations to build and support career-development resources.

Manufacturing

Dream It, Do It

http://www.dreamit-doit.com/index.php

The National Association of Manufacturers and the Manufacturing Institute created the Dream It, Do It campaign to educate young adults and their parents, educators, communities, and policy-makers about manufacturing's future and its careers. This Web site introduces high-demand 21st-century manufacturing professions many will find surprising and worthy of serious consideration.

Cool Stuff Being Made

http://www.youtube.com/user/NAMvideo

See for yourself how some of your favorite products are made compliments of the National Association of Manufacturers.

Manufacturing Is Cool

http://www.manufacturingiscool.com

Get a behind-the-scenes look at how some of your favorite products are manufactured at this Society of Manufacturing Engineers Web site.

Marketing
Take Another Look
http://www.careers-in-marketing.com/
Here's where you'll find links to all kinds of information about opportunities in marketing.

Science, Technology, Engineering, and Math (STEM)
Project Lead the Way
http://www.pltw.org
This organization exists to prepare students to be innovative, productive leaders in STEM professions.

Transportation, Distribution, and Logistics
Garrett A. Morgan Technology and Transportation Futures Program for Ninth through Twelfth Grade
http://www.fhwa.dot.gov/education/9-12home.htm
Get moving to find links to all kinds of interesting transportation career resources.

Index

Page numbers in **bold** indicate major treatment of a topic.

A

achievement (work value) 19
Active Software Professionals
  Alliance 47
Adams, Scott 6
Agrow Knowledge 177
AIGA 74
Amazon 140
American Health Information
  Management Association
  89
American Society for Quality
  125
America's Career InfoNet 176
America's Job Bank 176–177
Animation World Magazine 137
Application Development
  Trends 47
applications developer **47–49**
Army Intelligence and Security
  Command 66
arsenalexperts.com 79
Artificial Intelligence:
  Manufactured Minds 50
artificial intelligence scientist
  50–52
Association for Computing
  Machinery 59, 128
Association for the
  Advancement of Artificial
  Intelligence 50
Association of Database
  Developers 68, 71

Association of Support
  Professionals 131

B

baddesigns.com 130
Baseline magazine 101
BEST Robotics 110
b-eye-network.com 53
brainden.com 128
brighthub.com 95
build-flow.com 48
burgessforensics.com 79
business intelligence analyst
  53–55
businessintelligence.com 53
businesspundit.com 83
buzzle.com 107

C

caloriecount.about.com 75
Campaign for Nursing Future
  179
Career Builder Web site 177
Career Clusters Interest Survey
  26
Career OneStop—Students and
  Career Advisors 176
Careers & Colleges Web Site
  176
Careership 177, 178
Careers in Business Web site
  178
Careers in Finance Web site 174
casualconnect.org 143
Certified Ethical Hackers 67

chief information officer (CIO)
  56–58
Chief Information Officers
  Council 56
CIA triad 92, 95
CIO (chief information officer)
  56–58
CIO Magazine 56
CIO Update 56
college.gov 102
CompTIA 62
computer.howstuffworks.com
  62, 80, 88, 108
computer programmer **59–61**
computer repair technician
  62–64
Computer Security News 65
Computer World Security
  Topic Center 104
Confucius 121
Construct My Future 178
Consultant Coach 98
Consulting Magazine 98
Cool Stuff Being Made 180
Coward, Noel 2
"crackers" 67
creator (work style) 13, 14, 16
csoonline.com 95
cyber attacks 93
cyber intelligence analyst **65–67**
cyber theft 92

D

Dark Web 65
Database Administration
  Newsletter 68

database administrator **68–70**
databaseanswers.org 2, 71
Database Journal 68
database modeler **71–73**
Databases for Beginners 68
databreaches.net 105
data visualization specialist
  74–76
DBC Consulting 129
DECA 95
Developer.com 47
dietfacts.com 75
Digital Forensics Association
  77
digital forensics expert
  77–79
disaster recovery analyst
  80–82
Disaster Recovery Planning
  from A-Z 80
Discover Nursing 179
discovery.com 92, 104
Discover You at Work 5–42
  #1 Who am I? 8–9
  #2 What do I like to do? 10–11
  #3 Where does my work style
    fit best? 12–16
  #4 Why do my work values
    matter? 17–19
  #5 How ready am I for the
    21st-century workplace?
    20–24
  #6 "Me" résumé 25
  #7 Where can my interests
    and skills take me? 26–36
  #8 Which career path is right
    for me? 37–40
  #9 Career résumé 41
doer (work style) 12, 14
Dream It, Do It 180

E

earnings data
  applications developer 47
  artificial intelligence
    scientist 50
  business intelligence analyst
    53
  chief information officer 56
  computer programmer 59
  computer repair technician
    62
  cyber intelligence analyst 66
  database administrator 68
  database modeler 71
  data visualization specialist
    74
  digital forensics expert 77
  disaster recovery analyst 80
  e-commerce entrepreneur
    83
  hardware engineer 86
  health informatics specialist
    89
  information security
    specialist 92
  information technology
    auditor 95
  information technology
    consultant 98
  information technology
    project manager 101
  intrusion detection analyst
    104
  network administrator 107
  robotics software engineer
    110
  robotics technologist 113
  search engine optimization
    specialist 116
  simulation designer 119

  social media manager 122–
    124
  software quality assurance
    analyst 125
  systems analyst 128
  technical support specialist
    131
  technical writer 134–136
  3-D computer animator 137
  usability specialist 140
  video game designer 143
  video game sound designer
    146
  Webmaster 149
e-commerce-digest.com 85
e-commerce entrepreneur
  83–85
eCommerce Merchants Trade
  Association 83
Economic Stimulus Act (2009)
  76
edcollins.com 128
EHR (electronic health records)
  90–91
elearningexamples.com 74
Electronic Evidence
  Information Center 77
electronic health records (EHR)
  90–91
The Electronics Club 62
Electronics Project Design 62
e-mail 155
Enron 78
entertainment.howstuffworks.
  com 137
Entertainment Software
  Association 143
entity-relationship model
  (ERM) 72
epicsound.com 147

ERM (entity-relationship model) 72
evolver.com 137
ex-designz.net 131
Experiment with Success 153–174
Explore Health Careers 179

F

Facebook 122–124, 155
fbi.gov 105
Federal Emergency Management Agency (FEMA) 81
51 Coolest Robotics Blogs 110
filmsound.org 146
Finding Nemo 139
FIRST 110
fonerbooks.com 62
forbes.com 162
Forensic Focus 77
forgefx.com 119
freepctech.com 108
fun, work as 2

G

gamesounddesign.com 146
Garrett A. Morgan Technology and Transportation Futures Program for Ninth through Twelfth Grade 181
Google 85, 116, 117, 150, 151
govinfosecurity.com 65
greatdaygames.com 65

H

hackers 67
hardware engineer **86–88**

Health and Human Services, U.S. Department of 179
health informatics specialist **89–91**
helper (work style) 15, 16
hicareers.com 89
history.com 126
howstuffworks.com 62, 80, 88, 108, 113, 117, 137
hubpages.com 124

I

IBM 52, 63, 75
identitytheft.info 105
inc.com 162
The Incredibles 139
independence (work value) 19
Independent Computer Consultant Association 98
Information Management.com 71
information security specialist **92–94**
information support and services 45
information technology auditor **95–97**
information technology consultant **98–100**
information technology project manager **101–103**
infosecurityanalysis.com 105
InfoWorld Security topic center 104
Intel 59
interactive media 45–46
interest inventory 26–36
International Institute of Business Analysis 128

intrusion detection analyst **104–106**
investigation.discovery.com 92
ISACA 95
IT Security 92

J

javvin.com 86
Jeopardy! 52
Junior Achievement 95
Justice, U.S. Department of 96

L

lemonadegame.com 119
Listorious 124

M

madehow.com 126
Make It Happen 178
Manufacturing Is Cool 180
martymodell.com 128
mashable.com 122
maxi-pedia.com 95
mfgcrunch.ning.com 126
money.cnn.com 162
Monster.com 57, 177
Museum of Science (Boston) 113
My Arts Career 178

N

NASA Career Corner 110
National Association of State Chief Information Officers 56
National Center for Simulation 119

National Partnership for Careers in Law, Public Safety, Corrections and Security 180
Navy Center for Applied Research in Artificial Intelligence 50
network administrator **107–109**
Network Professional Association 107
network systems 45
networkworld.com 79
news.discovery.com 92
nobelprize.org 86

O

Office of Naval Intelligence 66
Office of the National Coordinator for Health Information Technology 89
O*Net Hospitality and Tourism Career Cluster 179
onlinebusiness.about.com 83
onlineschools.org 59
organizer (work style) 15, 16

P

Pathways to Technology 180
persuader (work style) 15, 16
Pixar 138
PlainLanguage.gov 134
Practical eCommerce 83
programming and software development **44–45**
Progressive Grocer 54
Project Lead the Way 181
Project Management Institute 101

pseudo code 111–112
Public Service Careers Web site 179

Q

QA Tutor 125

R

RDBMS (relational database management system) 68
ready.gov 80, 81
recognition (work value) 19
Recorded Future 65
recovery.gov 76
relational database management system (RDBMS) 68
relationships (work value) 19
RFF Electronics 129
rinkworks.com 65, 131
Road Trip Nation 156
Robotics Industries Association 110, 113
robotics software engineer **110–112**
robotics technologist **113–115**

S

Savio, Kathleen 78
science.discovery.com 104
science.howstuffworks.com 113
SC Magazine for IT Security Professionals 92
Search Engine Marketing Professional Organization 116
search engine optimization specialist **116–118**
Serious Games Challenge 143

seriousgamessource.com 143
simulation designer **119–121**
social engineering 94
social media manager **122–124**
Social Media Today 122
Social Networking and Media Association 122
Society for Technical Communication 134
softwareqatest.com 125
software quality assurance analyst **125–127**
soundsnap.com 146
SQL (structured query language) 68, 70
Strategic and Competitive Intelligence Professionals 53
styles, work 12–16
Supermarket News 54
support (work value) 19
survival-quiz.com 80
systems analyst **128–130**

T

Take Another Look 181
TechNewsWorld 86
technical support specialist **131–133**
technical writer **134–136**
thenetworkadministrator.com 107, 131
thinker (work style) 12, 14
3-D computer animator **137–139**
21st-century skills 20–24
Twitter 122–124, 155

U

usability.gov 142
Usability Professionals
  Association 140
usability specialist **140–142**
useit.com 150

V

values, work 17–19
video game designer **143–145**
video game sound designer
  146–148

W

Washington Post 65
Watson (IBM) 52
Webby Awards 149
webconfs.com 116
webdesignerdepot.com 74
Web Developer's Virtual
  Library 149
Webmaster **149–152**
WebProfessionals.org 149
Web sites 45
Web Standards Project 150
Wordpress 150

working conditions (work
  value) 19
Working Mother 162
work styles 12–16
work values 17–19
"Worst Software Blunders"
  47

Z

zEnterprise 63
Zynga 144